WANTED!

Bob Turney has become well-known as a writer, commentator and broadcaster on law and order topics. His book *I'm Still Standing* (1997) tells of his experiences 'at the wrong end of the law' and about how he turned his life around to overcome dyslexia, dependence on the 'safety and security' of prisons and hospitals, drug addiction and alcoholism - including a phase as a street drinker. He is also co-author, with Angela Devlin, of *Going Straight After Crime and Punishment* (1998).

In 1997 he obtained a degree from Reading University before joining Thames Valley Probation Service. He worked first in a hostel, then as a generic probation officer and later as a member of a youth offending team. He is now a freelance consultant and lives with his wife, Sue, and their five children in Reading. Bob Turney now devotes his spare time and energy to helping other people and his own brand of restorative justice: encouraging offenders to see that every offence has a victim and to leave crime behind.

WANTED!
Bob Turney

Published 2005 by
WATERSIDE PRESS
Domum Road
Winchester SO23 9NN
Telephone 01962 855567 UK Local-call 0845 2300 733
E-mail enquiries@watersidepress.co.uk

ISBN 1 904 380 13 1

Copyright © 2005 Bob Turney

Illustrations © 2005 Kara Gibson

Printing and binding Antony Rowe Ltd, Chippenham and Eastbourne

Cover design © 2005 Waterside Press

North American distributors International Specialised Book Services, 920 NE 58th Ave, Suite 300, Portland, Oregon, 97213-3786 USA

Also by Bob Turney

I'm Still Standing
1997 ISBN 1 872 870 58 9

Going Straight After Crime and Punishment (with Angela Devlin)
1998 ISBN 1 872 870 66

WANTED!

Bob Turney

Foreword by **Baroness Helena Kennedy QC**

WATERSIDE PRESS

Acknowledgements

In the first place I must acknowledge both Sue Turney and Anthea de Carvalho for the tremendous effort and considerable amount of time they have spent proof reading the manuscript, in order for it to be in a suitable condition to be sent off to the publishers.

Thanks must also go to Bryan Gibson and Jane Green of Waterside Press for their advice and editorial skills while working on the manuscript.

Also much appreciation goes to Baroness Helena Kennedy QC for her continuing support over the years, plus all my friends from church who are too numerous to mention by name, but each has shown a keen interest in my writing career.

Most importantly, my gratitude must go to my family who have given me undying support, not only with my writing, but with the other projects I have been involved in over the years.

I have been privileged to have worked with many people - some have been well-known, and there have been yet others who have been anonymous - but all have had a major influence on my life.

Thank you to all my friends and colleagues in the National Probation Service who have always been supportive of my endeavours.

Last - but not least - thanks to my Jack Russell, 'Bizzo' - for all the long walks he has taken me on to help me clear writer's block!

Bob Turney

April 2005

Foreword by Baroness Helena Kennedy QC

Bob Turney is an extraordinary individual. He suffered an appalling childhood and spent some twenty years in prison. Yet he not only survived these misfortunes but emerged a stronger person. He was so determined to become a decent and upstanding citizen that he conquered addictions to drugs and alcohol and overcame the disadvantages of a poor education. He was wrongly labelled 'subnormal' - when in fact he was dyslexic, unable to immediately recognise and associate words and letters - and his teachers wrote him off as 'quite useless'. This is the same person who later in life gained a degree in forensic social work, qualified as a probation officer and wrote a number of books - one of which became a set text for university students!

Bob has now worked as a probation officer for upwards of fifteen years - as he describes it 'putting back into my community some of what I once took out of it'. Many adult prisoners and particularly young offenders can be grateful to him for his work in helping them 'go straight'. These are not the easiest people to convince and they often say, 'It's okay for you, Bob - but it's different for us'. But he tells them that if he can do it then anyone can, even if they have to survive each day as a new challenge. He tells them to concentrate on the future whilst learning from the mistakes of the past - and to refuse to hear people who place obstacles and discouragement in their way. The process by which they leave crime behind is complex and difficult, but changing the mind-set of offenders is the nub of it. Bob's ideas have also come to stand for other things: hope, optimism, drive and motivation.

In his first book, *I'm Still Standing* Bob recalled how he turned his life around. It has been used in many settings - not just with prisoners - to demonstrate to anyone touched by disadvantage, deprivation or misfortune that they can overcome it. This message, as explained by Bob, has spread internationally and he now makes frequent trips abroad to speak on the subject as well as being in demand at home as a commentator on law and order issues. After reading that original book, the late Sir Stephen Tumim wrote that he was 'rather against the idea of prisoners . . . becoming professional former prisoners' but that Bob Turney was an exception. This was because Bob had devoted his life to helping people with problems of drink and drugs and had done a great deal of good.

I'm Still Standing ended at the point where Bob was about to study at university. *Wanted!* takes up where that earlier book left off, with Bob contrasting his new life with the lives of the people he knew in the past. He describes how in the 'second half' of his life he went on from university to put back into society some of what he once took out of it - a kind of restorative justice. The book also contains further insights and fresh perspectives for those of us within the criminal justice arena - and all the time his progress is recalled in the same laconic style and with the same self-deprecating humour as before.

When the Longford Trust was formed a few years ago, Bob was invited to become one of its patrons. Through this and similar involvements in the sphere of criminal justice he is now able to play an even greater part in influencing thinking, strategies and policies relating to offenders. In a sense, this is what this new book is all about: being wanted for himself, his ideas and the message of hope that he brings to other people - not constantly living on the streets and being wanted by the police as was once his lot in life. Bob Turney's story is one of redemption; and it defiantly challenges those who believe that punishment is the only viable response to crime.

Helena Kennedy

April 2005

Prologue

I wrote this book at a time of unparalleled change in the UK's criminal justice and penal systems - a time of extraordinary events when hardly a day went by without some new development, not least the resignation of a Home Secretary and the longest session of the House of Lords for a hundred years - and to deal with a law and order issue![1] 'May you live in interesting times' goes the ancient Chinese saying. We certainly do.

Like many people working within the system, I have felt the wind of change on almost every front. If it is not new sentencing powers, it is prison building, new detection methods, alliances between the various criminal justice services or fresh targets of one kind or another.

• • •

There used to be hardly a mention of these kinds of things in the newspapers or on TV. They were discussed behind closed doors and were largely the province of beaurocrats, not politicians or the media. Things did sometimes hit the headlines particularly when something went seriously wrong. In *Chapter 6* I talk about the tragic case of Craig and Bentley when the media was suddenly full of opinions about how to deal with offenders. The same kind of publicity followed the Great Train Robbery that is the subject matter of *Chapter 7*.

Nowadays, law and order is high on the agenda and often way out in front: deaths in custody, drugs, guns, knives, violent crime, binge drinking, anti-social behaviour, paedophiles, identity theft, organized crime and 'cybercrime' (the label given to crime on the Internet). These are the kind of issues that now pervade my life whether during 'A Visit to Number Ten' (*Chapter 1*), 'On the Speaking Circuit' (*Chapter 4*), 'In the Media' (*Chapter 5*) or back at the office dealing with some of the day-to-day matters that I mention in *Chapters 8* and *9*.

I suppose that open government makes for democratic government but it can also be unsettling. To stay on 'home ground' - my old 'profession' burglary - in 2004 a man was stabbed in a struggle with a burglar in Chiswick, west London and another fatal stabbing by an intruder followed soon afterwards in another part of the city. Such events are very rare indeed: but within days the right to defend one's home had become a high profile political issue. Sir John Stevens, the outgoing Metropolitan Police Commissioner, told *The Daily Telegraph* that when seeking to defend their homes 'homeowners should be

---

[1] Concerning Government proposals for control orders in relation to suspected terrorists.

presumed to have acted legally, even if a burglar dies, unless there is contrary evidence' and added that 'individuals should only be prosecuted when there is evidence of gratuitous violence'.

Homeowners have always been entitled to use 'reasonable force' to defend themselves and their homes and at the end of the day juries have decided what level of force is reasonable in given circumstances. But a campaign to protect householders further had been ignited. Before he left office, Home Secretary David Blunkett MP indicated that he favoured increasing that protection.

All this caused the penal reform, victims, civil liberties and human rights groups to weigh in with their views - and as is frequently the case whenever burglary is in the news I was contacted by reporters. I told them that I doubted any change was necessary. It had always been pretty clear to me what 'reasonable force' meant and I was sure juries made allowances for the spur of the moment reactions of householders acting from fear and under pressure who happen to pick up some normally innocent item like a cricket bat to defend themselves. The debate really began five years earlier following the case of the Norfolk farmer, Tony Martin, who was sent to prison after shooting dead a burglar at his remote farmhouse - and there had also been a case in Florida, USA in which a British tourist who knocked on the door of a house to ask for directions was mistaken for a burglar and shot dead.

Reasonable force does not mean that someone can 'lie in wait' for an intruder or use disproportionate force or chase after intruders in retaliation. A householder cannot dispense summary justice or lynch law. I mention 'folk hero' Tony Martin and the 'hangers and floggers' in *Chapter 4* and again in *Chapter 8* when I look at 'Restorative Justice'.

• • •

I told everyone who contacted me that - as a responsible citizen - if I found an intruder in my own home I would naturally do my utmost to protect my family and my belongings. Like anyone else I would use whatever means were to hand to protect my family from harm. But only to the extent of using *protective* force. I am not going to chase after someone in revenge. I would call the police and let them deal with it. One reporter said that I was 'flying in the face of popular opinion'. Most people wanted the right to use a greater level of force and not to be answerable to the courts simply for going over the top.

But did they? I doubt it. Certainly the new Home Secretary, Charles Clarke, having taken a cooler look realised that the law is perfectly workable without it being changed. He was supported in this by several leading lawyers including the Director of Public Prosecutions. In a novel move the Government issued an explanatory leaflet for householders - although whether people will actually study it or simply keep it by the bed in case remains to be seen! We were told that, in practice, very few prosecutions arise out of the use of excessive force in such circumstances and that in 2003 only five householders had been found guilty as a result of doing so - and only one of these was sent to prison for any length of time. But with law and order now so high on the agenda everyone had to be made to feel uneasy for a while.

• • •

An endless round of radio interviews and appearances also led me to think how fickle the media can be. I was invited onto one late night panel discussion on BBC Radio Five Live to discuss the Government's decision not to change the law of self-defence and protection of property. All keyed up, I arrived to discover that the programme had been put back because news was breaking that Prince Harry had attended a fancy-dress party dressed in a Nazi uniform. Priorities! Conscientiously and in order to be even more prepared I spent an hour making notes and was looking forward to a heated discussion with people who I had been tipped-off held views that were very different to mine. By the time we were due to go on air I was chomping at the bit. But this was only to discover that by now everyone present - the presenter, press representative and senior police officer - were all now in agreement with the new Home Secretary's decision. The programme thus largely consisted of us patting each other on the back and telling each other how right we all were!

Similarly, over the years, I have learned not to take everything I read in the newspapers too seriously. One reporter phoned to ask if I had had any photographs taken when I was beaten up! When I tried to explain that I was not a *victim* of burglary but an ex-burglar who now works within the system 'on the side of law and order' and who sometimes comments on such things, she became insistent. Surely her source could not be wrong! She did eventually phone back to apologise for 'a complete mix-up'. Another thought that I was the spokesperson for burglars generally, a sort of union representative.

Then *The Times* published a menacing picture of me next to the headline 'Don't Take Them, Urges Former Thief' - the implication being that I was standing up for the burgling fraternity. What I actually said is that the Home Secretary could sleep soundly in his bed knowing that 'Bob the Burglar' agreed with his decision! Next day *The Telegraph* went one better printing a similar picture beneath the headline, 'Meet the

Worm that Turned'! That's a new way of describing 'going straight', I thought.

• • •

In the pages that follow I have tried to give a flavour of 'what has happened to me' since the time when *I'm Still Standing* was published. That book ended where I was about to go to university. At the time I was just grateful that I had escaped my past and had survived to lead a normal life 'on the outside'. I had no great aspirations or ambitions other than to keep it that way. But things took a further turn. Before long I found that I was 'wanted' by all kinds of people, mostly to do with the fact that I had made the leap from offender to ex-offender and was prepared to try and explain this to people: to pass on my thoughts about how others could rise to the challenge - to give them a message of hope and encourage them to make a leap of faith.

Up until that point I had only ever been wanted by the police and some of the most nefarious people you could ever wish to meet!

To Sue, my eternal companion

WANTED!

CONTENTS

Acknowledgements *vi*

Foreword by Baroness Helena Kennedy QC *vii*

Prologue *ix*

Chapter

    1 A Visit to Number Ten *15*

    2 What on Earth Has Happened to Me? *31*

    3 Frank *39*

    4 On the Speaking Circuit *53*

    5 In the Media *63*

    6 Capital Punishment *79*

    7 The Great Train Robbery *101*

    8 Restorative Justice *121*

    9 What on Earth will Happen Now? *133*

CHAPTER 1

A Visit to Number Ten

CHAPTER 1

A Visit to Number Ten

The fast, inter-city train to London gives me half an hour to think. I can set the old grey matter working in preparation for the day's events. On a normal day, the trip may be for a meeting or conference - or to attend The Old Bailey or some other Crown Court. I may be visiting a prisoner in my role as a probation officer to talk about things that will affect his or her entire life - the possibility of a long sentence or being let out on parole. Then again, I might be heading somewhere to give a lecture or after-dinner speech. More and more often these days, my appointment is to do with the media where the focus on crime and punishment has never been so high. I describe all these things in the chapters that follow.

• • •

This time it was completely different. I am not sure what was going on inside my head. I know I was full of apprehension - too keyed up to think, read or even take in the scenery. I had been in this state on and off ever since the invitation arrived. With luck the butterflies would go away before we reached Paddington Station.

Once in London, I took a deep breath and resolved to put on a brave face. I made my way over to the taxi rank, queued for five minutes and then climbed aboard a waiting cab. Boldly and confidently - as if I had been doing it every day of my life - I told the driver, 'Downing Street, if you please'.

'You're not one of "Tony's cronies", are you, Guv?' said the cabbie after a long pause.

'No, no, no . . . I'm heading for a reception . . . it's being hosted by Cherie Booth, the Prime Minister's wife'.

There was another long pause. He must have been thinking 'Yes, clever Dick. I know Mrs Blair uses an alias, but who the flipping heck are you all dressed up to the nines!'

I was wondering the same. I knew I had come a fair way since I was released from prison for the very last time twenty-five years earlier, but here I was about to arrive at one the best-known and most significant addresses in the world. Who the flipping heck was I and what was I doing here? Whatever had happened to me since those far off days? As we edged through the traffic - the driver putting the world to rights and me nodding politely - I stared out of the window and began to survey the map of my life. I was Bob Turney, ex-burglar. That was what my imaginary calling card said. That was the description that should have been on the guest list and that was what the toastmaster should have called out when I entered the room: 'My Lords, Ladies and Gentlemen, Mr Bob Turney, ex-burglar'!

My thoughts were abruptly halted by the cabbie telling me that we had arrived in Whitehall. I settled up and he said, 'Give my love to Cherie'. I smiled and answered, 'Of course'.

I walked the short distance to the gates of Downing Street, showed a policeman my pass and was let inside. I made my way to the police portacabin and emptied my pockets into a tray for inspection before stepping through the X-ray machine. I knew the routine. I was no stranger to security procedures. I had submitted to being searched many times when I was a prisoner or when I was accused of 'loitering with intent' all those years ago. It is also a frequent practice nowadays at many of the prisons I visit as well as when people go into major public buildings.

Gathering up my things, I made my way to the front door of Number Ten. The policeman standing outside saluted me.

'Good evening, Sir.'

I smiled and returned the greeting, glimpsing for just a moment a picture of the days when I would have tried to run him and his colleagues breathless after being caught red-handed. It was my main fitness regime at the time!

I walked in, took off my overcoat and an attendant placed it on a coat hanger. A man in a morning suit approached, 'Mr Turney, please come this way'. Deferentially and with an outstretched hand he indicated the direction in which I should go - up the staircase lined with photographs of former prime ministers. Taking a moment to absorb my surroundings and the grandeur of the place, with its chandeliers and paintings hanging on luxuriously decorated walls, I thought to myself, 'I really must do something about my offending behaviour. Just look where it has landed me now!'

• • •

I stepped into the reception room where the Great and the Good were starting to gather and took a glass of orange juice from a tray held out by a waiter. I have not touched alcohol for twenty years. 'Twenty years dry' as those of us who cannot handle the stuff call it. I started to mingle. I gladhanded my way around the room whilst waiting for the speeches to begin. The room was literally bubbling with a hundred conversations which became louder the more the drinks circulated. The air was thick with the odds and ends of a dozen and one disjointed conversations.

'They solve everything with DNA nowadays...'
'Tell me, how many times have you written to the Lord Chancellor about it now..?'
'They made a hospital order...'
'Three police officers and two private security guards...'
'So what happened is that the magistrates made an anti-social behaviour order...'

'They're hoping for a public inquiry...'
'Wait until you see the next British Crime Survey...'
'They're trying it out in Warwickshire, Devon and Brixton...'
'Is the report out yet..?'
'Didn't she publish an article in the *New Law Journal*...?'
'Three strikes and you're out...'
'There was a marvellous piece in *The Guardian*...'
'They put him on Rule 45 the minute he arrived...'
'When does the statute actually come into force..?'

'Have you met . . . he's just back from a restorative justice conference in Ottawa . . . They're way ahead of the game. '

'Have you seen the latest circular on electronic tagging?'

I made a beeline for Ann Widdecombe MP. It was the time when Michael Howard had just been elected Leader of the Opposition. Jumping straight in at the deep end, I asked her whether she still thought that he had 'something of the night' about him - a remark she had made publicly when he was Home Secretary and she his junior minister and which probably cost him the Tory leadership at that time. The witticism relied on the common Romanian link that features in both his family origins and those of Dracula, the legendary vampire. She smiled diplomatically and replied, 'No comment'. I admire her. She has a rare quality and sticks to her principles. We are miles apart on penal reform, but that is quite another matter. The American singer Donny Osmond was touring Britain at that time and was about to appear in London. He was keen to meet with 'people of influence' and I had been given a couple of backstage passes. I grasped the opportunity and invited Ann to come along with me. Unfortunately she already had a fixed engagement on the evening in question and was quite disappointed. That would have been a claim to dine out on: that I once took Ann Widdecombe to a Donny Osmond concert! Instead all I am left with is the boast that I was once stood-up by her. Michael Howard might say the same thing, but it would carry a quite different meaning!

• • •

Very soon the assembled guests were shown into the adjoining room where Cherie Booth was waiting to welcome everyone individually. My turn came and as we shook hands I was tempted to say, 'Where's Tony? Is he putting the kids to bed?' but resisted the thought. The event was to mark the achievements of the Prisoners Education Trust and we chatted for a short time about the way in which I had benefited from an albeit somewhat late (but, as it turned out, excellent) education.

As I made my way around the room, my mind started to contrast the Downing Street guests with what I once mistakenly took to be high society in those distant days when my only ambition was to prise myself upwards from the lower rungs of the underworld ladder. My friends in those days came from an entirely different social stratum and my inter-personal skills rested more on the crumbs of my failed attempt to become a boxer than on guides to etiquette. As for 'people of influence' and the like, my idea of power was that there were certain villains who had risen to the top of the pile and called the shots. Big spenders who mostly lived in houses with electric gates and whose only pets were guard dogs. As for politicians I cannot remember that we paid them much attention - except that is at election time. Then we would find out where the candidates lived and look to see if there might be any pickings whilst they were away on the campaign trail. I remember that one year we discovered that the MP for Sutton in Surrey lived in a big house near Cheam. Whilst he was 'out for the count', so to speak, we turned the place over.

My early adult life was populated by people you would not want to meet on a dark night. Eddie, for instance, was a well-known local villain. I once made a comment about his wife, saying, she looked 'like a bulldog chewing a wasp'. Eddie got to hear about this and was not pleased. A couple of evenings later I was sitting at the bar having a quiet drink, when, all of a sudden, there was a loud bang as the swing doors at the end of the room were kicked open. Lo and behold, it was Eddie! He stood in the doorway, wearing a long black coat, doing a great impression of Clint Eastwood. All that was lacking was for the jukebox to be belting out the theme music from 'The Good, the Bad and the Ugly'.

Eddie began to walk towards me, his eyes bulging like organ stops. He was an angry man. Halfway across the floor, from under his coat he produced a sawn-off shotgun and began to shout obscenities at me. I started to laugh when over his shoulder, I saw my mate Terry creeping up behind him with a large ice bucket. Terry smashed it down over Eddie's head, following which Eddie could not see a thing. Terry then picked up a bar stool and hit him with it a couple of times, which knocked Eddie to the floor. He lay there, with the bucket over his head and the shotgun by his side, looking for all the world like Ned Kelly. Terry and I then made a speedy exit through a different doorway, just moments before the police came streaming in like the Keystone Cops. They arrested Eddie, who was still incapacitated.

In the early 1970s, when colour TVs were just coming online, Terry and I took up stealing them to order. We were never short of customers and the supply was never ending. We were overwhelmed with 'orders' and even had a waiting list! We were stealing up to four sets a day and getting up to one hundred pounds each for them - a lot of money in those days. We even gave a warranty and provided an 'aftersales service', using a moonlighting service engineer who went round sorting out any problems. However, I treated this source of 'income' as nothing more than a kind of voucher system that kept me in alcohol and drugs - it bought me a nightly ticket to oblivion and that was all. I had no comprehension of the value of money in ordinary terms. Even at the level I was coining it in, I was permanently 'skint'. I would be making two hundred pounds a day and only a few pounds would be left the next morning - if I was lucky - mainly because I was always partying the night before.

We once ram-raided a TV shop (though it was not called ram-raiding then). I reversed the van through the shop window and we stole four state-of-the-art colour sets. The following evening our raid was featured on the BBC TV programme 'Police Five' and the presenter, Shaw Taylor, mentioned that our loot could be leaking radiation. This was in fact not the case, but in those days TV sets *did* have a small black box at the back containing a miniscule amount of radioactive material, though not enough to harm anyone. But the broadcast really laboured the point about how dangerous the stolen sets were. Within minutes I had my first 'customer' demanding his money back and asking me to collect the set we had delivered earlier under the warranty so that he did not have to touch it. Before the week was out we had been obliged to buy back all the rest: we could not shift them for love or money and - in the days when I would not have recognised pollution if it had risen up and whacked me in the face - we ended up dumping the whole lot in the river!

In our partnership, Terry and I had defined roles. He would find the houses to break into and I was the 'wheels man', the one who would lay on the transport. I always had various stolen vans dotted around the area ready for use. One day he said he had 'a right little earner' but we would need something big to move the stuff in. I left him in our usual watering hole and set off to see what I could find. The only thing that fitted the bill was an ambulance, so that is what I was driving when I returned to pick him up. When we arrived at the scene of the intended crime we were a bit conspicuous - and there were plenty of curtains twitching as we edged along the road. But it was a big house, with a long drive and no one from the road outside could see what we were up to. Once we had loaded what we came for, I drove off at high speed with the blue light flashing and the siren going full blast. Everyone gave way!

Some twenty years later, when my first book was published, I gave a number of media interviews. My publishers received a call from the BBC saying that 'someone from my past' had seen me on TV and wished to contact me. I wondered at first if someone was looking to settle an old score and was initially apprehensive about this voice from the past. But then the BBC said that the man's name was 'Terry'. We had lost touch in the past. Still a little anxious, I picked up the telephone and rang the number that they had given me. It was the selfsame Terry. His voice was unchanged, but, like me, he had undergone a spiritual conversion. Just as I had become involved in my church he had also - but even more so - he was now a minister of religion. So we have renewed a relationship that had ended when I was sent to prison, but on a very different plane to how it was all those years ago.[1]

Another and more dubious character from my old social milieu was 'Mad ' Ronnie Fryer. He lived up to his name. In the 1960s he spent time in Broadmoor special hospital, on the basis that he was criminally insane. He had been 'nutted off', as they say. Mad Ronnie lived a couple of streets away from me and was one of the most psychopathic people I ever had the misfortune to meet.

Many petty criminals in my area went into hiding when Mad Ronnie was around. The atmosphere would change completely if he walked into the public bar. People would avoid making eye contact with him in case he misread an innocent look; they would keep their heads down in case he came towards their table and if he did decide to join them they would have to buy him 'rum and pep' for the rest of the evening. If anyone said anything that he did not like, there would be trouble. He was always 'tooled up' and spoiling for a fight.

---

[1] Terry Mortimer's story became one of those featured in *Going Straight After Crime and Punishment* by Angela Devlin and Bob Turney, Waterside Press 1998.

I remember on one occasion walking into The Rose public house in Shepherds Bush one Sunday lunchtime to be confronted by Ronnie, holding a gun to the head of another local villain. The blood had drained from the poor guy's face, whilst Ronnie's was bright red and the veins in his neck were sticking out. The next thing I saw was the pair of them starting to laugh as Ronnie let go of the guy and put the gun back in his pocket. They then carried on drinking like old pals. 'Whatever was all that about?' I thought - but no one asked questions when Ronnie was about!

Another time I was having a few drinks with some of the lads when Ronnie decided to join us. After a few rum and peps he began performing his party trick: eating a whisky glass. He sat there munching on the glass with blood pouring from his mouth. I was frantically thinking of an excuse to leave without upsetting him because it looked as if trouble was on the horizon. You always knew he was in that sort of mood when he started eating the glassware. I made a big thing about having to make a telephone call from the payphone in the lobby and managed to slip out the back door without being noticed.

In those days there was a Greek café in Shepherds Bush and in the back room were held illegal card schools. Sometimes Ronnie would visit the café for a few hands. The Greeks were not lacking in the old grey matter - they would let him win until he got the money he needed so that he would then leave. That was all well and good until one evening Ronnie got into a game with a stranger who did not understand this basic rule. All hell was let loose when Ronnie started to lose and the guy finished up with even more scars on his face than he had when he arrived. No one dared go to the police.

Mad Ronnie would later kill Terry Marsh. Marsh was a friend of Joey Pyle, who I say more about in *Chapter 7*. On the morning of his murder, Terry Marsh had given Joey a lift to Gatwick Airport. Later that day, Ronnie turned up at Marsh's used car lot and an argument kicked off between the pair of them, as a result of which a fight broke out and Ronnie took out a knife and stabbed Marsh in the heart. He then went 'on his toes' but the word on the street from Joey Pyle was that positively no one was to help Mad Ronnie to stay on the run so Ronnie was soon picked up by the police and remanded in custody to Brixton Prison. Knowing that the odds were that he would never be released, his thoughts turned to suicide. He pleaded with his wife, Maureen, to smuggle in some cyanide pills by stitching these into the lining of a jacket that she handed in at the prison when she took Ronnie a change of clothes. Even the police felt sorry for Maureen and she was not charged with any criminal offence.

Following Ronnie's death, things began to loosen up on the outside and return to 'normal'. People began to resurface and The Rose attracted customers again, but it was not long before trouble broke out. It could have been a coincidence but it seemed as if Mad Ronnie might have been receiving protection money from the landlord, and now he was not around to keep an eye on things standards were deteriorating. So the landlord employed four bouncers. Needless to say, this caused a deal of resentment amongst us regulars, who all felt that the money would have been better spent paying us to keep order! So we decided to show the landlord that the bouncers were not all they were cracked up to be.

One evening I was in The Rose drinking with a few lads and all of us becoming increasingly confident about how we could handle ourselves as the evening went on - especially as one of our group was a professional heavyweight boxer. We hatched a plan to pick a fight with one of the bouncers and then blame them for causing trouble. Seeking to create an impression, I volunteered to pick the fight, even though the bouncers were all massive guys each standing over six feet tall and weighing around eighteen stone - whereas I was a good deal shorter and eleven stone even when soaking wet.

'If I have to go out, I'm going out in style,' I thought to myself. I noticed that one of the bouncers wore a syrup ('syrup of fig' equals wig) so I asked the barmaid if she could fetch me a salt cellar from the kitchen, which she did. I walked over to the bouncer and sprinkled some salt on his shoulders. 'There you go, mate, that will make it look more realistic ... it looks like you have got dandruff on your shoulders!'

The bouncer was furious and made a grab for me. In a split second, I saw my whole life flash before me, thinking that the end was nigh. But as the bouncer was about to chin me the boxer stepped in and delivered a devastating right hook, sending the guy's head rolling back, dislodging the syrup and causing his eyes to roll as he dropped to the floor, bald as a badger. He was out cold. All hell broke loose and it was like a scene out of a John Wayne film with tables, chairs, bottles and glasses flying through the air and things smashing everywhere. I was lucky to emerge unscathed.

Next day the bouncers were all sacked and they had to close down The Rose for a couple of days while it was spruced up again. The police hit a wall of silence. They questioned people for a few days afterwards but no one had seen anything, no arrests were made and even the landlord was not willing to talk. After that, he employed some of us and the place ran comparatively smoothly.

Scamps was a local nightclub and - always looking for advancement - I got wind that they paid their bouncers ten pounds a night plus all that they could drink. That really appealed to me. I kept pestering the manager for a job, but he was not having any of it because my reputation as a drinker and pill popper had gone ahead of me and I was not the sort of person he wanted patrolling his premises. But shortly after 'The Battle of The Rose', which had become the talking point for miles around, I was in Scamps having a drink within earshot of the manager and dining-out on tales of the big fight, grossly exaggerating my own involvement in sorting things out. He must have lost his senses because he came across and offered me a job. I could not believe my luck: free drinks and getting paid for the privilege cash in hand at the end of each night's work. It was a dream come true for me!

The following evening I turned up at Scamps in a black suit, white shirt and black bow tie, my shoes highly polished. One of the regular bouncers showed me the ropes. My own first priority, of course, was to get stuck into the free drinks. And - just to make the evening go with a swing - I went into the back office where I popped a couple of pills. I cannot remember a thing that happened after nine o'clock, never mind two in the morning. I woke up around lunchtime with a massive hangover, sore ribs and a nose that hurt like mad and seemed to wobble from side-to-side when I tried to blow it. There was blood on my shirt and the buttons had disappeared along with the bow tie. 'All part of the job,' I tried to convince myself, 'and I don't doubt that the manager will give me my wages in the morning as he must have forgotten last night'. As soon as I was back on my feet I legged it down town to buy fresh evening wear.

When I turned up for work that evening I was met at the door by two of my bouncer colleagues who took me by each arm and frog-marched me into the manager's office. I noticed that he too had a black eye. The look on his face told me that he was less than happy: 'You're fired, Turney! I pay my staff to stop fights not to start them'.

• • •

Someone else who I ran into occasionally was Jack 'The Hat' McVitie. He was called 'The Hat' because he was never seen without one, having lost most of his hair at an early age. The rumour was that he wore it in bed because no matter what time of day people called around at his house he always had it on his head, even at breakfast. Years later he was murdered on the orders of the infamous East End gangsters Ronald and Reginald Kray who took charge of the underworld in the 1950s. The story goes that they had paid him a hundred pounds (five thousand by the standards of today) to kill Leslie Payne, a one-time associate of theirs who had 'fallen from grace'. Jack was no better. He pocketed the money but did not keep his side of the bargain. Then, stupidly, he got high on drugs and alcohol and began spouting about how he would get the Krays. His days were numbered from then on.

There was always high speculation about what happened to The Hat's body. Rumours abounded in the pubs and clubs that his remains had been smuggled into a hospital and disposed of in the incinerators, or buried in concrete inside a motorway support column, or fed to pigs at farms the length and breadth of the UK, depending on the latest whisper and who you listened to. My favourite was the tale that The Hat was placed 'two up' in a coffin and cremated along with its other occupant in full view of the unsuspecting mourners. Needless to say, when that story was doing the rounds there was never any want of underworld heavies claiming to have been one of the six pallbearers and hoping to curry favour with the Krays. I have it on sound 'authority' that the truth is that The Hat's body was driven to a remote spot on the Kent coast where a friendly fisherman tied it round with lead weights and dumped it overboard half-way across the English Channel.

I suppose that what I once took for the high life was in fact the worst form of lowlife. I often shudder when I think about it - but it is almost like it happened to someone else. Since those days, my friends and social contacts have changed entirely and my way of life has changed too in almost every respect. Not that I have my own butler or valet yet! But it does mean that I am not quite so filled with 'the three As' - awe, anxiety and apprehension - when an invitation drops into the mailbox.

• • •

I attended another reception at Number Ten that was given to acknowledge the work of Frank Longford, whom I talk about at length in *Chapter 3*. He had such an effect on my life. After he died, his family and a few friends got together to set up a charity in his name, the Longford Trust, and they invited me to become a patron, which I gladly accepted. There is now also a Longford Lecture on a topic related to the trust's aims and objectives. The first of these was given by Cherie Booth herself. The following year it was given by the Bishop of Birmingham, John Sentamu, and in the third year by Archbishop Desmond Tutu of South Africa. I say more about this in *Chapter 8*. There is a corresponding Longford Award that is presented to someone who has made an outstanding contribution to social or penal reform. The trust is also setting up a fund to offer financial assistance to ex-prisoners who wish to move into higher education.

I remember on that occasion having a long one-to-one conversation with Cherie Booth in which we dissected the probation service and reconstructed it on the spot. I told her I believed the service was in decline and would not exist as we know it in a few years' time. The general public has been encouraged to have less and less faith in what it is trying to achieve with offenders - and many people think of probation officers as 'wishy-washy liberals' who care only for offenders and not for victims of crime. This is untrue of course, but it is a stereotype that is magnified by certain sections of the media. The headlines then shout out that this or that criminal has 'walked free' from court, when what has really happened is that he or she has been given a tough and demanding community sentence. Clearly there is an important job to do explaining this to the public and the fact that we really do need to make choices about how resources are used in terms of crime prevention.

Perhaps community sentences need to develop greater credibility with the public and offenders alike - and maybe they will do so under the umbrella of the new National Offender Management Service.[2] In *Chapter 8*, I talk about restorative justice which is also something that needs to be more properly and widely understood.

Cherie Booth asked me what I thought should be done, and I told her that there are very many offenders who *do* comply with the terms of their community sentences - including some people who have been persistent in their offending up until that point. If they do not complete their orders, warrants are issued for their arrest. The real question is whether the police give these enough priority and act on them so that the system as a whole remains effective. In many instances, it is only if someone is arrested for fresh offences that a warrant for non-compliance with an earlier community sentence is 'dug out' from the police files. I am sure that many probation officers would agree that this can make a nonsense of what they as a whole are trying to do.

We also agreed that probation officers should have 'teeth'. Not of the chopper variety but when it comes to the enforcement of community orders. Then we could concentrate on more productive work, directly with offenders - which serves to reduce re-offending rates, protect the public and save the taxpayer a great deal of money in the long run.

'My husband would be interested in hearing about that,' she said and asked me to drop him a line. I have found that the system survives on networking but you rarely get such a 'direct line'!

It was time to set off around the room and mingle with the other guests. We turned for the inevitable photograph. I am not photogenic. I regularly receive 'get well' cards or even condolence messages after my picture has appeared in a newspaper or magazine!

---

[2] The National Offender Management Service (or NOMS) was created in 2003 to oversee both the National Probation Service and HM Prison Service under the overall control of a single Commissioner of Correctional Services. This is part of widescale changes across the criminal justice system that are designed to improve matters all round.

I am pleased to say that the evening passed without major incident. There was no violence, no disorderly or anti-social behaviour and no-one was arrested for making-off with the silverware so prominently on display. But I was button-holed in a corner towards the end of the evening by a rather ruddy-faced individual who wanted to have a word in my ear about a 'friend' who was trying to come to terms with alcoholism. My lawyer and doctor friends tell me that it happens to them all the time on social occasions, people nudging them and describing 'someone else's' problems or symptoms and asking whether there is any advice that they can pass on. Nine times out of ten, so they tell me, that 'someone else' is the alter ego of the person asking the questions!

CHAPTER 2

What on Earth Has Happened to Me?

CHAPTER 2

What on Earth Has Happened to Me?

It can take just a split second for something to hit home. Like the time when I walked through the swing doors into the arrivals lounge at London's Heathrow Airport. In the distance on the other side of the barrier stood an executive chauffeur in his sober suit holding a piece of paper to his chest on which I could just decipher my name: 'Turney'. I had just arrived on a transatlantic flight after a short lecture tour in the United States. I was carrying my hand luggage and pushing a heavy trolley. My laptop computer was slung over my shoulder and my mobile phone was at the ready. As the signal settled I quickly pressed the dial-up button and waited for my wife, Sue, to answer.

'Hello.'

'Hello, I'm back . . . I'll see you in half an hour . . . But, Sue, I'm standing here about to be whisked off in a limousine by a guy in a peaked cap and there's folk staring at me from every side trying to work out if I'm somebody important. What on earth has happened to me?'

'Bob . . . You've arrived!'

● ● ●

I had *arrived*. We were just into the new millennium, and with a new century seemed to come a new life. I can't remember exactly when I first realised this but there was definitely a moment in time when it happened. I arrived in the real world and left my past behind. Being picked up like royalty was just the icing on the cake and it brought home to me just how far I had travelled, in life as well as on the aeroplane that I had just left.

In the past, I had asked myself so many times over the years, 'Whatever will happen next?' As a child the question was always at the forefront of my mind and one that I frequently asked myself in my loneliness and despair. It was there during the nightmare of my schooldays when I suffered bullying at the hands not just of the boys but also of my teachers. It was there when I was labelled 'educationally subnormal' and later 'dyslexic' and also after I had subsequently come to believe entirely in my own uselessness. I was always anxious: I needed to know that I was not just on some slippery slope that would eventually lead to my complete downfall. Years later, when Birmingham University adopted one of my books as a core text on a criminology course I thought back to those times and said to myself, 'Now tell me I'm subnormal!'

On leaving school I had been barely capable of writing my name and never did learn to spell my address properly, because of my as then unrecognised dyslexia. I seemed to have spent most of my childhood quivering at what might happen next as part of a highly dysfunctional family headed by a manic-depressive father who insisted on dominating day-to-day life with his mood swings. In my adolescent years I fell into alcohol abuse, drug addiction and petty crime, which led to me spending the best part of twenty years drifting in and out of a string of prisons and institutions. Eventually, I had ended up in a psychiatric hospital following a desperate but typically incompetent suicide attempt. It continued like that until I woke up one morning and realised that things just had to change. It was not an easy transition and the thought of what was to come, that I might somehow end up in an even worse mess, was always there at the back of my mind. Even now, I still need reassurance, especially when life takes a new turn as it had on this occasion. As I stepped out of the airport I could easily have been mistaken for an international businessperson who was travelling back and forth every other day. I needed reassurance about tomorrow.

In the past, I never seemed to acquire much that you would describe as being 'for the long term'. It was largely 'easy come, easy go'. Each time I left prison it was straight off down the pub or to renew my arrangement with the local drug-dealers. Until the money ran out. Then it was back to the suburbs where the same vicious cycle of offending, arrest, imprisonment and release would begin all over again. Prison was an occupational hazard. When I was inside I did not have to think too hard, or worry about a roof over my head or what was for dinner. Once I knew the ropes and had learned to keep my head below the parapet I felt safer on the inside than on the streets. But once on the outside the anxieties would begin to build up once again. Where to sleep; what to eat; where the money was coming from and how I was going to keep back the thoughts that would plague my mind about what was going to happen in the future. More drink, more drugs to hide the misery and the pain. I had become a real champion at feeling sorry for myself.

• • •

Getting out of the rut was a long, slow process, which I dealt with in detail in my first book *I'm Still Standing*. To put things in a nutshell, it meant overcoming alcoholism, drug addiction, dyslexia and a deep-seated lack of self-esteem. That long phase of my life ended as I began to study for a degree in forensic social work at Reading University. Later, after qualifying, I was fortunate enough to find a job with Berkshire Probation Service - now called Thames Valley Probation Service - where, ironically, several of the people who had once acted as my probation officers when I was an offender became my bosses, line managers, colleagues and friends. A strange turn of events!

I worked first in a probation hostel and later, after finding my feet and gaining experience, as a member of a local youth offending team - or 'YOT' - which I still do. People who work in the system love acronyms and abbreviations, but I still have the edge when it comes to the alien and exotic language of prison, which I can still speak like a native! The idea of a YOT is that people with a range of different professional backgrounds, skills and experience - probation officers, youth workers, police officers, education workers and so on - get together as partners to work out the best way to deal with a youngster.

The things I learned whilst doing my degree combined with the remnants of a streetwise attitude (which I sometimes demonstrate by over-emphatically talking out of the side of my mouth and putting on a macho swagger known on the inside as a 'bowl') seem to have served me and the young people I work with well. I do not think I come over to them as an authority figure or part of the establishment and I think this helps to build bridges and make connections with those who feel alienated, hopeless or who fear the future themselves.

Another side of my new life has seen me on the speaking circuit and appearing in the media commenting on issues to do with crime, justice and penal affairs - which is what took me to America, where I have now been many times - as well as across Europe. I have been 'wanted' if you like, in my job, on the lecture trail and by the press and TV - and in an entirely different way to that in which I used to be wanted by the police in my youth!

By the time my chauffeur was pushing the trolley laden with suitcases across the road outside and towards the car park, I was already engrossed in a further telephone conversation with a TV producer who wanted me to appear on his chat show.

'My diary is completely full for the next few weeks.'

'How about six weeks' time?'

'Not much better, I have to be at work *some of the time* . . . I've just been away from my desk for nearly three weeks!'

'How about a TV link or failing that a pre-recorded interview then . . . we can splice you in?'

By now we had reached the waiting car where the driver held the door open for me and looked towards me with the same fixed expression on his face that I used to use when kowtowing to a prison officer. I only hoped that he was not thinking what I used to think. The TV producer was becoming persistent, promising me the earth, and pandering to my ego - as they tend to do with everyone!

As I made myself comfortable in the back of the car and we sped off towards the M4 motorway, I reached into my travel bag and began to look at my schedule for the next four weeks. It was truly manic - I had speaking engagements at both Eton College and the Oxford Union to debate law and order issues, as well as an after-dinner speech at the House of Lords! Within the next couple of days I would need to put together a thousand words for my regular column in the local newspaper and a film producer wanted to talk about making a documentary about my life. Somehow I had to return to my full-time job as a probation officer and pick up on the clients and cases that I had asked a colleague to cover whilst I was abroad.

Eventually and to get it out of the way, I agreed with the TV producer to do a short recorded interview over the weekend before I returned to work, even though it would mean another trip to London and whilst I was still jet-lagged. 'I'm not sure if I will be up to it', I told her but it did not seem to have the slightest effect. Arrangements were made for the BBC to send a car for me.

I also had to touch base with Frank (Lord) Longford who was keen to hear how the talks I had given in America had gone and about what I had discovered there. I suspected that there would be a grilling concerning *how bad* things are with their system! So the next couple of days would see me filming my interview at Wormwood Scrubs Prison in Shepherds Bush and lounging in the bar of the House of Lords for a chat with Frank about the horrors of American justice. Two days earlier I had been exchanging opinions with leading judicial and academic figures on the far side of the pond. That is how chequered and interesting my life has become. No wonder I was beginning to wonder what on earth was happening to me.

• • •

I had to fit in a further visit to another prison later that same week. My 'old nick', Wandsworth Prison were holding a fundraising event for the Prisoner Education Trust and I had agreed to do a presentation. The audience included senior judges, leading barristers, magistrates, prison staff and police officers. Chairing the event was the Bishop of Wandsworth who introduced me. I got to my feet and began:

> I'm told the best way to start a talk is either with a joke or a lie. Well I'm afraid, ladies and gentlemen, I do not know any jokes, but I must say that you're the most intelligent looking bunch I've seen in a long time!

I spoke for forty-five minutes and the event raised much needed cash. I eventually arrived home around midnight feeling shattered, got into bed and fell sound asleep. The following morning I called into my local radio station to review the newspapers and was on the air for a good twenty minutes. Then it was off to the office as usual to start my day's work with the YOT. I count myself lucky to be doing a job that allows me to make a contribution to the community in which I live and to put something back. I see it as a counter to the days when the only contribution I made was to the crime figures!

It is an incongruous image. An ex-con in a suit and tie ruminating on the problems of crime and punishment: but it usually takes only seconds to break the ice. A few self-deprecating comments soon serve to demonstrate the angst and sense of futility of the unsuccessful criminal – and they just love it when I tell them that I was not even good at being bad. Failure heaped upon failure and with self-respect at its lowest ebb.

It is through such snapshots of my earlier and seemingly inescapable lifestyle that I am able to show people what is really involved in coming back 'from the depths' and so give hope and encouragement to others.

I remember telling the inmates at Wandsworth Prison about when I got my first flat following years in institutions. I suffered for weeks from the inconvenience of having the bed in the lounge where the decorators had left it – because it never occurred to me that I was allowed to move it! That is the way prison affects people, especially those who have been locked up for a long time. Other people make all the important decisions for them.

• • •

If anything registers the extent to which life has changed it is a perfectly innocent quote by one of my former associates who, troubled about not being able to contact me for a day or so because I was so inundated with things to do, became quite critical of the fact that my new life was taking up so much of my time: 'The trouble with Bob Turney is that he has forgotten he used to be a criminal!' No longer one of us, I guess he was trying to say.

But I have not forgotten. One of the things about living on the edge is that it reminds you all the time how thin the veneers of success, respectability and indeed society are. It can easily fall apart unless you work at it each and every day. I have not forgotten living in a rat infested squat in Wimbledon; my life was a mess, my alcohol intake and drug abuse long since out of control. My life had deteriorated to the point where I would drink and take drugs until I passed out. I could be comatose for days just lying in a filthy room on an old mattress on the floor. There I would lie, fully clothed, bathed in my own vomit and urine.

I was making a rapid descent into oblivion and I knew that it was only a matter of time before I died a lonely death and it would be days before anyone would discover my body. I woke up about ten in the evening once, the place freezing cold. I already felt like death warmed up and I despised myself for what I had let myself become. I managed to get to my feet and staggered out onto the street. I needed a clear head and some food inside me. The only place I knew where I could get that was in prison. I managed to cross the road and started kicking in the front door of a tobacconist's shop. It was not long before the police obliged and I was arrested. By lunchtime I had been sentenced and was safe inside Brixton Prison.

You never forget things like that.

CHAPTER 3

Frank

CHAPTER 3

Frank

Frank Longford - Lord Longford always insisted that I call him just plain 'Frank' - opened lots of doors for me that would otherwise have stayed firmly shut. Once, after listening to one of my presentations, he suggested that I should go and talk to the boys at his old school, Eton College. 'That would be interesting,' I replied, 'someone once labelled "a dunce" and "educationally subnormal" lecturing to pupils at one of England's top public schools!' I thought nothing further of it. To my astonishment, a week or so later I received a letter inviting me to address the Eton sixth form.

• • •

I approached the college's magnificent buildings nervously, knowing, among other things, that Prince William would be in the audience. I was met by one of the masters who took me on a tour of the school before I was shown into the main lecture theatre, where around five hundred boys sat row upon row in their celebrated morning suits.

I began the presentation with a story I once heard Sean Connery tell about his childhood in the back streets of Edinburgh. He said that he had not known he was living a deprived life until social workers turned up one day and told him so! I then compared my own childhood explaining that I grew up assuming all fathers attempted suicide at regular intervals, after which they would spend several weeks in a psychiatric hospital before being sent home - where the same cycle of recovery, high spirits and depression would begin all over again.

'I wouldn't mind betting you're pretty tired of being told that you come from privileged backgrounds', I challenged my audience, '. . . and I'm sure at least one of you will be thinking, "Doesn't everyone live in an imposing house surrounded by cast iron railings with a posh flag flying from the roof?!"' This brought a roar of laughter. I continued by telling the boys about my life drifting in and out of prison before I did a complete U-turn. They seemed to grasp my allusion to poachers and gamekeepers, especially when I apologised for not wearing tweeds and a Barbour jacket. I told them what it was like being an ex-offender who was hell bent on going straight, how I managed to persuade the education authorities to let me study at university and how eventually I had become a probation officer dealing with the very kind of people I used to be myself.

'It was an effort becoming accepted by ordinary, decent people... Had I known I was going to go straight I would have got my parents to put my name down for it as soon as I was born!' Another roar of approval. We were from different worlds but we were somehow managing to connect. By the time I had thrown in a couple more anecdotes the nerves had disappeared completely. I told them about *my* schooldays and about being diagnosed as 'dyslexic' - which caused me to worry for weeks on end about my sexual orientation - and about my fitness regime: being chased by policemen and acting as a bookie's runner. But there were also serious points that by now they were listening to intently, never knowing when the next self-deprecating story would be slipped in.

It was a fascinating experience and there was a string of questions when I finished speaking, not to say the odd interruption, which is always a good sign whatever the audience. I have been invited back several times and delight in telling people that 'I went to Eton' even if it was only for a morning. If I really want to wind people up I add that I 'went on to Oxford'. Oxford Magistrates' Court that is, to hand in a pre-sentence report!

After my talk I was invited to join the boys for lunch in hall. As I tucked into my roast beef and Yorkshire pudding I soaked up the grandeur of the place and reflected on the famous Old Etonians who had once graced those tables - from poets to prime ministers. The place was so grand and I was so inconsequential sitting there beneath the stained glass windows and chandeliers. I was having one of my 'Whatever on earth is happening to me?' turns. I pictured myself twenty years earlier, alone and freezing cold in some dimly lit prison cell or trying to sleep off the after effects of cheap alcohol on a park bench. It was also a million miles away from the dining-room of my old south London comprehensive school with its distinctive aroma of vacuum packed cabbage - and light years on from the dishing out of 'gruel' on prison landings during my days as a guest of Her Majesty. Gladly, these thoughts were soon gone and I rejoined the genial conversation.

Nowadays my visits to Eton and the links that I have with the staff and students there always remind me of Frank and the good and loyal friend that he became.

• • •

I met Frank Longford for the first time by chance in the early 1990s when he visited a probation hostel in Reading. He just popped in! When he heard about my journey across the tracks, he invited me for lunch at the House of Lords. This was the first of the many times we sat down together to sort out the world of prisons and imprisonment and how to deal with offenders. I think he was fascinated by the fact that I had made such a radical switch - studied me like a specimen in the laboratory - and did everything he could to make sure things stayed right side up for me. Despite my own anxieties and concerns, he had complete faith in my potential. He insisted I *could* do things. He had a knack of bringing out the best in me and other people. I have seen him do it many times. He had the gift of being able to motivate lost souls. He constantly encouraged people and was always ready to actively assist them in whatever way he could. Quite remarkable, especially as the years rolled on.

Although he and Myra Hindley are both now dead Frank will be forever linked with - some people would say 'tarnished by' - the fact that he campaigned so robustly for her release. She was the most demonised woman in British criminal history and speaking up for her was always going to be a thankless task. But he did so with gusto as he did whenever he sensed injustice or that someone was a victim of the system. The hatred that many people seemed to have for Hindley merely acted as a spur to him. Working closely alongside him - as I was fortunate enough to do from time-to-time - I came to understand a good deal about the kind of person he was and what drove him.

Many of us who were around at the time can remember just what we were doing on the day that John F Kennedy, the US president, was shot dead in Dallas by Lee Harvey Oswald. It is the same with the deaths of Elvis Presley, John Lennon and Princess Diana of Wales or September 11, 2001. Events like these have a strange way of registering in the psyche. Likewise, I can also vividly recall where I was when the verdicts in the

'Moors Murders' trial hit the newsstands. I had just caught a tube on the Northern Line of the London Underground at Morden, heading for Tooting Broadway. On the opposite side of the carriage sat a middle-aged man reading the *Evening Standard*. Staring out from the front page were photographs of Ian Brady and Myra Hindley and the simple, bold headline 'GUILTY!'

The same photographs have since been reproduced thousands of times, especially that of Myra Hindley with her peroxide blonde hair and menacing stare. The murders shocked the nation and became a benchmark by which many other acts of so-called 'evil' came to be judged.[1]

How society deals with horrific crimes is always problematic and these were horrific by any standard. It is not only about what to do with or to the offenders but a communal sense of guilt that they could have happened at all, which needs to be assuaged in some way. Lesley-Ann Downey and John Kilbride were both strangled. Edward Evans had been attacked with a hatchet first. But what made the case even more notorious was a tape-recording played to the jury of Lesley-Ann pleading for her life. The tabloids waged a campaign of hatred against Hindley in particular - and as with the Penny Dreadfuls or broadsheets of old, rage and disgust made good editorial copy and sold countless newspapers. It was also in the media's interest to keep up a 'drip effect' and to recycle the story at intervals afterwards. Not surprisingly, the hysteria seemed to increase whenever the question of Hindley's release was mentioned - whether by Frank (or, occasionally, by someone else). The issue became a poisoned chalice for a succession of Home Secretaries: one by which an entire political career or law and order strategy stood to be judged.

At the trial both the defence and the prosecution agreed that Hindley was Brady's 'lieutenant'. The trial judge, Mr Justice Fenton Atkinson - who naturally had all the evidence to hand plus his direct personal observation of Hindley in court - made an objective judgment about the length of time she should serve in prison. Two days after the trial, he wrote to the Home Office stating that he believed Brady was 'wicked beyond belief' and with no hope of redemption 'short of a miracle'. He did not think the same about

---

[1] In 1965 after a fifteen-day trial at Chester Assizes, Brady and Hindley were each jailed for life for the murders of Lesley-Ann Downey, aged ten, and Edward Evans, aged seventeen. Brady was also convicted of murdering John Kilbride, aged twelve, and Hindley found guilty as an accessory to that murder. The bodies had been buried on Saddleworth Moor near Manchester and hence the unforgettable soubriquet the offences attracted with its remote and Satanic undertones. Twenty or so years later, Hindley and Brady confessed to two further murders of which they had long been suspected, those of Pauline Reade, aged sixteen, and Keith Bennett, aged twelve. They were never charged with these crimes. Hindley returned to Saddleworth Moor with the police to help them locate the body of Pauline Reade, but that of Keith Bennett was never found.

Hindley, once removed from Brady's influence. In his opinion, he wrote, she should remain in prison for 'a very long time'. He recommended that her 'tariff' - the minimum time that she should spend in prison for the purposes of punishment and retribution before being considered for parole - should be fixed at twenty years. Soon afterwards, the Lord Chief Justice of the time, Lord Lane, recommended that this be increased to twenty-five years. Later home secretaries increased her tariff to thirty years, then to 'whole life', meaning, in effect, that she became one of only two dozen prisoners in the UK who could expect never be released. After she had already served ten years more than the twenty recommended at her trial, the then Home Secretary Michael Howard reaffirmed the whole life tariff. A heavy smoker, she was to die of cancer at the point where the legitimacy of these procedures was being challenged under European law. Had she lived much longer she would undoubtedly have become a pawn in a larger political battle.

So why, if she *was* just Brady's 'lieutenant' and acting under his influence, did Hindley come to take centre stage? Frank's explanation was typically uncomplicated: this was the one modern instance in British criminal history of a woman being convicted of serial sexual killings involving children. How could a *woman* do such a thing? Women are considered to be life givers not those who take it away. Even if they do not actually give birth, society expects them to embrace the qualities associated with womanhood and motherhood, such as nurturing and protecting children. Although this may nowadays be seen as a discriminatory approach or stereotyping, Hindley flew in the face of that image and was thus a 'monster' in the eyes of the public - led on by the tabloid press. Her crimes undermined a belief in the 'basic goodness' of women. So great was the original public outrage that a petition with 30,000 names was collected calling for the death penalty to be reintroduced.[2]

There was little focus on the fact that Brady and Hindley were lovers to the extent that either of them might behave in bizarre and - especially for Hindley - untypical ways when in each other's company. As Helena Kennedy QC writes in the first edition of her book, *Eve Was Framed* (Vintage, 1992):

> Women find themselves in the criminal justice system for two reasons, one is because they haven't got a man in their life, and the second is because they do have a man in their life.

---

[2] Ironically, in 2000, when Ian Brady began a hunger strike in a bid *to kill himself* and challenged the right of the authorities to forcibly feed him there was a different outcry with various people and organizations arguing that he should not be allowed to commit suicide.

With Hindley this seemingly eternal truth appears to have been particularly acute and magnified several times over. Yet, strangely, much of the strongest opposition to the idea of Hindley being released came from other women perhaps due to the empathy they felt for the mothers of the murdered children and a strong sense of sisterhood and 'shared grief'. Such attitudes die hard. Sue and I have tried to raise our children in the Christian tradition, including so far as principles of repentance and forgiveness are concerned. Yet, even today, if someone were to ask our twenty-four-year-old daughter, Sarah, what should have happened to Myra Hindley she would let you know in no uncertain terms, including in her view that people like Hindley should not be released.

Geoff Knupfer, the detective chief superintendent in charge of the investigation into the Moors Murders - including the questioning of Brady and Hindley - has stressed that Hindley was acting under the powerful influence of Brady. He went on to say that he saw no reason to doubt that - *if they had never met* - she would have led a normal life, marrying and raising a family like any other woman from her background. Even prosecuting counsel at the trail, Elwyn Jones QC (later Lord Chancellor), accepted that Hindley had been 'indoctrinated' by Brady.

In the end, Hindley died from natural causes, still in prison thirty-six years after her sentence began and having been turned down for parole many times. Peter Stanford summarised the still widespread hostility towards her in the *Guardian*:

> There are a small number of Christian names that have been out of use because of their association with one hated individual. In Germany, Adolfs under fifty are thin on the ground. And you can count on the fingers of one hand how many Myras were born in this country since 1966.

Crimes involving children as victims naturally provoke a sense of anger in the great majority of us - but Frank's case was that Hindley had become an emblem for all such offences, rather than someone who was being judged as the individual that she was, or had become whilst in prison. He argued that it was important in a democracy that espouses human rights that offenders, whoever they are, do not come to represent something else entirely or find themselves being subjected to disproportionate treatment.

• • •

It was Lady Ann Tree, who had been visiting Hindley in Holloway Prison, who first contacted Frank about the case. She knew of his longstanding interest in penal reform and that he himself had been visiting prisoners since the early 1950s. To begin with, she asked him if he could 'lend weight' to representations being made to the Home Office to allow an inter-prison visit between Hindley and Brady. Frank being Frank, not only agreed to help but threw one hundred and ten per cent of his efforts into his friend Ann's request. His efforts were to no avail, but he did start visiting Hindley in 1969 and so the media vilification that existed towards her was extended to include him, as one of most bizarre relationships ever - that between a peer of the realm and a serial killer - blossomed. That friendship was to last into three decades.

Throughout the 1970s and the 1980s Frank withstood a torrent of abuse, especially in the tabloids who nicknamed him 'Lord Wrongford' and pigeonholed him as 'a loony peer' and misguided eccentric, given to lost and unpopular causes. Those of us who knew him personally know better. He was a charismatic man with a keen sense of humour who drew people like a magnet. For me, he was also the personification of a Christ-like life and his faith was unwavering. He was a man of great integrity and when he said that he would do something he did it.

What made Frank a cut above the rest of us and gave him a freedom to behave as very few people can or are allowed to, was the sheer strength of his beliefs and the fact that he really did not care what people thought. He was passionate about what he perceived to be the injustices of life. Political Correctness was something that passed him by; and he was never afraid to speak his mind or call a spade a spade.

Frank's dress sense left a lot to be desired. He usually wore a threadbare suit that the local Oxfam shop would not have returned a thank you for, along with a pair of worn-out trainers. His hair went untended. When he came to the launch of my first book, *I'm Still Standing*, one of the guests did not recognise him at first. He thought that I had invited one of my old street-drinking companions as some sort of publicity stunt.

The broadcaster Jon Snow, whose first job involved working for Frank, once said of him that he was both 'the battiest and the most intelligent man' he ever knew - my own sentiments also. But for me the statement that rings truest is that Frank was a friend to the friendless.

He was the author of a number of books. One story repeated in his presence many times but which he would neither deny nor confirm was that after he had written a book about humility he went into a leading London bookstore and demanded to know why it had not been placed in a more conspicuous position in the window! He it was who coined the description 'Prince of Darkness' for the then Home Secretary Michael Howard long before it became common currency. He is also reputed to have said, after being told about the death of a member of the House of Lords: 'How could they tell?'

He often received hate mail from the public and his reputation as a Labour politician and a reformer was assailed on all fronts. But this simply increased his determination. I once ran into him in the lobby of the House of Lords. He had a copy of the *Sun* tucked under his arm and I asked what he was doing with such a dreadful newspaper. 'I'm just keeping tabs on what the enemy is up to', was his reply.

Less well-publicised is the fact that Frank often visited Ian Brady.[3] But it was Frank's association with Hindley that led to the greatest condemnation. Peter Stanford wrote some words in Frank's biography, *The Outcast's Outcast* (Sutton, 2003), that I think come close to answering the question 'Why did he adopt such unpopular causes?':

> Frank's approach to prisoners had long been based on the refusal to sit in judgement and an unconditional offer of forgiveness and friendship whatever their crime. It was his unshakeable belief that no prisoner was beyond redemption.

Whilst in prison, Hindley had returned to the Catholic faith of her teenage years and it was Frank's and her shared belief in Catholicism that brought them close together. He once referred to her in the media as 'a good religious woman' - and he could not understand that the public would not take his word for it that she was a reformed character.

• • •

At one stage, Frank's efforts to calm the media and public opinion were actually having an adverse effect and eventually Hindley began to plead with him to 'ease up' with what had become a highly visible campaign. He appeared on 'Kilroy' - the BBC TV morning discussion programme - when he abandoned any appeal to reason and came out with the bald statement that anyone who did not believe Hindley should be released was stupid! She, in turn, tried to distance herself from his antics, by now seeing her hopes of release put in jeopardy by a loose cannon. The publicity he was generating was backfiring.

His friends also suggested that he take a back seat and allow others like the Reverend Peter Timms, a former governor of Maidstone prison, and Lord Astor, one-time owner of *The Observer*, to continue with the campaign. Theirs was a more subtle approach - and from what I knew of Frank subtlety was not his strong point! He retreated reluctantly, since he always saw it as his mission to persist with whatever he believed in to the bitter end. By the early 1990s he had stopped visiting Hindley altogether. They

---

[3] He once told me that Brady was 'one of the most intelligent men he had ever met'.

would exchange birthday and Christmas cards, and occasionally she would write to him but that was all.

In the spring of 1998 I met Frank at the House of Lords. I had been helping with some research for a speech he was to deliver in the House. He was in high spirits. He had just received a letter from Myra asking him to visit her at Highpoint Prison in Suffolk. He said that he and his wife Elizabeth would be going.

As they were both by now aged over ninety, it would have been a nightmare of a journey for them by public transport. They would have had to get from their Chelsea flat to Liverpool Street Station, then take a train to Ipswich before changing for Bury St Edmunds, from where it would have been a thirteen-mile taxi ride to Highpoint. Nonetheless they were willing to take this on. Without hesitation I offered to drive them there and before he could say, 'I can't put you to all that trouble, Bob', I insisted. I saw this as an opportunity to do an anonymous good turn, working on the principle that helping out without people knowing about it would be that much more meaningful and perhaps earn for me some kind of merit in the hereafter! So I was economical with the truth. I arranged for someone to cover my probation duties and told Sue that I was going on 'a prison visit'.

After an early start I found myself in London by nine o'clock, where I picked up Frank and Elizabeth. It was a warm, spring day as we set off through the city centre heading east. We stopped off at a pub for lunch. Frank was easily recognisable from his unkempt appearance and famous pebble glasses but sometimes people could not immediately put a name to the face. A couple of barflys kept looking over at us with puzzled expressions on their faces. Eventually, curiosity got the better of them. Rising from his stool one of them came over to where we were sitting and said to Frank, 'You're that lord, aren't you . . . that lord who's been in the papers?' Quick as a flash Frank replied, 'Yes, that's right . . . I'm Lord Lucan'! By now, the customer had an even more perplexed look on his face as he retreated to the bar. He began an argument with his companion as to who Lord Lucan was and by the time we were ready to leave things were getting heated and the barman had joined in. It was typical of Frank. Rarely could he make an exit without leaving a controversy in his wake!

In the mid-1970s, Highpoint was converted from a Royal Air Force establishment to a category B prison, or middle-ranking in security terms. Because of certain incidents of unrest and a series of escapes it earned itself the nicknames 'Knifepoint' and 'Hi-de-Hi-point' (after the TV holiday camp sitcom 'Hi-de-Hi'). It soon became evident that there had been a leak: as we drove up to the prison gate several photographers jumped out of the bushes and off went the flashbulbs.

Before I knew it, Frank was out of the car holding a press conference! I was helping Elizabeth out when I heard him say, 'I am not posing for any photos unless I have my friend with me' and before I knew it I was standing in front of the main gate of the prison flanked by the pair of them. One of the reporters called out, 'Who are you?' Desperately, trying to hold on to what little obscurity remained, I replied, 'I'm the chauffeur' - but Frank chipped in, 'He is far too modest. This is Bob Turney, my friend who is an ex-prisoner, and who is now a probation officer'. So bang went my 'merits'. He and Elizabeth went inside and I drove off for a while to avoid prying questions. An hour or so later I returned. The media pack had gone and I waited in solitude for the two of them to emerge.

The journey back to London was full of enthusiastic talk about what the next move should be in the campaign to free Hindley. This continued late into the evening in the bar in the House of Lords. It was a delightful outing even though my cover would be blown by the morning papers.

• • •

Frank always believed that Myra Hindley was treated wrongly in comparison to other life sentence prisoners or those who had committed heinous crimes. As early as 1985, her case was reviewed in the normal way by a local committee of the Parole Board, which recommended her release considering that she had served that part of her sentence necessary for justice and retribution and was no longer a risk to the public. The following year the Parole Board recommended that she be moved to an open prison – often a preliminary to being released on parole shortly afterwards. More than fifteen years later, when she died, she was still in much the same state of limbo. In the meantime IRA bombers who had killed women and children were being released following the Good Friday Agreement! The repeated decisions to keep her incarcerated were, Frank believed, largely influenced by a continued blood-lust amongst the tabloid press as it went about inflaming public opinion. He argued that Hindley's grounds for parole lay in the fact that she had rehabilitated herself and that she was no longer a risk of harm to the public. He said that it was clear from those who knew and worked with her that she fitted the criteria for release but that politics stood in the way.

Even Myra Hindley's body needed a police guard to prevent it being photographed or mutilated and the funeral took place in relative secrecy. Phil Woolas, the MP for Oldham East and Saddleworth, said: 'No one will miss Hindley; whilst nobody would wish anybody suffering and pain it is with a sense of relief that we can now begin to put this nightmare behind us'. More recently, similar sentiments have been directed towards Maxine Carr over her part in the Soham murders, even though she played a minor part in those events when compared with Hindley's role in the Moors Murders. Freedom of expression is one thing: but that way also lies the lynch-mob and the burning of witches.

• • •

Bernard Levin wrote once wrote in *The Times*:

> Everybody asks the wrong question about Lord Longford, viz., is he barmy? The question is not worth asking; of course he is barmy. What we should be discussing is something quite different: is he right? Of course he was right to stand up for what he perceived to be an injustice. Frank could never be accused of being a moral coward. He did not shy away from what he clearly believed was wrong. He was a latter-day David who tried to slay an insurmountable Goliath in the form of the media and public opinion, whilst I stood with some other metaphorical Israelites cheering him on from our hiding places.

I am sure that, given time, Frank Longford will be remembered as one of the great prison reformers of modern times. His greatest 'crimes' will come to be viewed as attributes: forgiveness, humility, understanding and humanity. His name will come to rank alongside those of John Howard, Elizabeth Fry and Alexander Patterson. He was sometimes accused by his critics of visiting only high profile prisoners and seeking to make political capital out of this. But let me at least put that part of the record straight. He would go and see anyone who asked him to do so. Even towards the end of his life he was visiting at least two prisons a week and several times that number of prisoners. He doggedly travelled thousands of miles, mostly by public transport. He also stayed in contact with the families and friends of prisoners - who, equally, often had to make long and arduous journeys, sometimes with small children, just to spend a couple of hours with their loved ones. Often Frank's and their return journeys would mean getting home late into the evening. He did this week-in, week-out for decades without a word of public thanks or acknowledgement.

For many years, he also visited one of England's most notorious 'hard men' - Charles Bronson - a lifer who adopted that name by deed poll. Bronson was - and still is - a body building fanatic and once Frank, by then in his mid-seventies, took up his challenge to get down on all fours and do press ups - with prison officers looking on in disbelief. Frank was only disappointed that he could not do the one armed version like Bronson!

Each year the Longford Trust - of which I am so proud to be one of the patrons - mounts an annual Longford Lecture, in association, so far, with *The Independent* newspaper. An annual award is given to an individual or organization that has made an outstanding contribution to prison or social reform. I have also been privileged to sit on the panel of judges. In 2004 we were going through the nominations when we came to a letter from Bronson nominating Frank himself for the award. It read:

> My nomination is a strange one, his truly 'Lord Longford' . . . For many years Frank stood loyal to me, he visited me in many jails. He even saw me in special cages. He saw me at my worst time and my best times. He must have travelled thousands of miles just to give me support. His advice was priceless, his humour was brilliant. His faith was incredible . . . We often fell out, he always came back. I at times sent him crazy messages. I once was very disrespectful. But he always had a smile for me. He trusted me. Why? God only Knows! He was often warned off from seeing me. One prison Governor refused to let him in to see me, owing to a 'bad day' (my bad day). He was kind to me. Honest and a true friend. He had even shed a tear on the odd occasion over my treatment. He saw me with black eyes and fat lips. He saw me soon after I had lost a loved one and he helped me to come to terms with my madness. Few ever showed me compassion, but Frank did . . . He treasured a photo we once had taken in Hull Gaol of us together. I am proud to have had him in my crazy life. I was proud of how he tried to make my quality of my life more humane, and often brought my case up in the House of Lords. After 30 years in jail, with 28 years of that spent in solitary, I am still in solitary. I can put my hand on my heart and say, 'I do miss the old git', he is irreplaceable. RIP.

Charles Bronson

CHAPTER 4

On the Speaking Circuit

CHAPTER 4

On the Speaking Circuit

I found myself sitting at the top table of the main dining-hall in the House of Lords wearing my dinner jacket and black bow tie. I had just finished a superb meal of roast duck with full trimmings, washed down with sparkling, ice-cold mineral water topped-off with a slice of lemon. It was a far cry from prison fodder collected from a serving trolley and eaten alone surrounded only by the four walls of a cell.

The Master of Ceremonies rose to his feet and I took a last sip of water to loosen my throat. He brought down his gavel three times on the oak table and in a booming voice announced, 'My Lords, Ladies and Gentlemen . . . Pray silence for your speaker this evening, Mr Bob Turney'. I gulped down a last mouthful of water, took a deep breath (which I find helps to quell the nerves), feigned my most villainous expression and pushed myself up out of my chair.

• • •

Earlier in the day I had been filming at Wandsworth Prison for a TV news item. My mind had flashed back to my time as a prisoner on A-wing - 'A3/36' to be exact, or cell thirty-six on the third landing: 'the threes' as they are often called. Beyond the prison wall, so far as I could tell, it was a damp and misty evening. It was February and the cell was freezing cold, even after I had climbed up on the chair to make sure the window was well shut. But it still let in the cold and a terrible draft through the cracks around its edges. It was like living in a refrigerator.

I was six months into a two-year stretch for burglary. I might as well have been in solitary confinement, since I spent most of each day locked in my cell with little to interrupt the boredom or solitude. At that time I could not read or write and I had not broken bread with another human soul for months. The highlight of the day was when I was allowed out for half-an-hour for exercise: once in the morning and once in the afternoon. Even when it was snowing it was warmer in the yard and at least I could step up my blood circulation by swinging my arms. We had to walk in a clockwise direction around the prison yard in pairs ('*with time, not against it*' being the tradition in UK prisons). But if the snow kept coming we would not be able to go outside and things got even bleaker. Our cell doors would be unlocked and we would have to walk around the ground floor - 'the ones' - which with the constant echoes of cell doors slamming, the dim half-light from the lack of windows and the stale air was about as dispiriting as things could get. At least when we were outside I could fill my lungs with fresh air and clear the stench of stale urine from my nostrils.

So I explained to the assembled Lords and their guests what the experience of being in prison was really like in those days. About how I took a blanket, wrapped it around my shoulders and sat on the hard iron framed bed, no higher than a stretcher and upon which there was the thinnest of mattresses. I told them about the bucket that served as a toilet in the days before 'slopping out' was made unlawful under human rights law and how I breathed into my hands to keep warm whilst waiting for the evening play to start on the radio. With luck and assuming that the well-used batteries lasted out, this would act as a distraction and transport me elsewhere for an hour or so.

As I scanned the plush surroundings, the thick carpet, wood panels, and scalloped cornices - and noted the general sense of well-being of those facing me from the elaborately decorated dinner tables - the contrast with my earlier life could not have been greater. But then neither could my life as a whole. Standing there to give that after dinner speech, I knew that I had now journeyed to the two poles of the social landmass - and I could not help sharing the thought with my audience: 'Oh dear', I said looking pointedly around the room, 'Just look where my offending behaviour has got me now!'

• • •

It is certainly not every day that I get to speak or dine in such fine surroundings. It might equally be in little more than a broom cupboard, with a group of young offenders whose motivation and aspirations when I begin are little higher than the skirting board. The 'speaking circuit' frequently taken me to prisons across the country, from Littlehey Prison in Cambridgeshire - a long drive across the flat fenland countryside to speak to several hundred prisoners, and hopefully somehow to inspire them - to regular haunts such as Pentonville, Wormwood Scrubs and my own *alma mater* Wandsworth Prison. I also vividly remember several trips to Holloway Prison in north London along with other writers such as Angela Devlin (my co-author on *Going Straight)* and where the women always gave us a rousing reception and send off. Then there are the many university campuses that I have been fortunate to visit for the same purpose - as well as visits to countless village halls, churches, youth clubs, police stations and even the Inns of

Court and the Oxford Union. There have also been my travels abroad, especially to the USA and Germany. It takes stamina to travel around in this way and can mean arriving home at all sorts of 'unsocial' hours and still with the need to be back at my desk by morning. It also means that I am regularly reliving past experiences for people and linking these to modern-day law and order issues.

• • •

The UK prison population is now around the 75,000 mark (and predicted to reach more than 90,000 within a decade, so that even though extra prisons are being built the accommodation is being 'gobbled up' as fast as it is being created). Thirty years ago, when I was serving my time, it stood at well under 40,000 - a figure then thought to be precariously high in terms of public spending, the management of prisoners and the risk of disturbances. There was always a shortage of prison officers, but what changes? Many people working in prisons will tell you that they are constantly up against targets, resources, budgets and the wind of change. Since my time also, law and order has become a major industry, with some sections of the community calling for people to be locked up as if it were a new pastime that could replace foxhunting: now that blood sports have been banned it could be the next best thing! I try to explain to my audiences how prison is often not the best answer and I try to support this from my own experiences and by tapping into a stockpile of facts, stories, anecdotes and embellishments that that I have built up.

Telling people about my own life is my way of illustrating a point and getting over to them why it was that I eventually made the effort to go straight. So I explain about how sometimes, when I was in prison - meaning on the odd day and if we were lucky - we would be put to work in the mailbag shop and made to sit in regimented rows sewing canvas sacks. At that time, a 'Rule of Silence' was imposed whenever we were at work. Talking to anyone was strictly prohibited and if we did so we could end up on a disciplinary charge with the prospect of our release being delayed when the time came because of 'added days', meaning extra days added to a sentence as punishment. These were dished out by a governor at a hearing called an 'adjudication' at which, given prison culture, we were expected to say 'Yes, sir, please, sir, three bags full, sir'. That system has now changed because the governor was held to be acting as prosecutor, judge and jury. At exercise, we *were* allowed to talk - but only to the person right next to us, not the prisoner in front or behind. We were also banned from putting our hands in our pockets even on the coldest of days.

We sewed sacks by hand: a regulatory five stitches to the inch. My fingers would be covered in blisters by the end of the day, but being out of my cell for a few hours compensated for that. On some evenings there were 'classes': whatever was available, usually using prison officers as instructors or teachers from the local technical college. At one prison I joined a class to learn Basic English. Initially, I volunteered because I thought it would break the monotony and, again, I would escape from my cell for a short time - and possibly be able to talk to other inmates because the rules about conversations were more relaxed in the classroom. This is how my dyslexia came to be discovered: but the sad part is that it meant that I had to stop going along. When I was a child I knew that I was stupid and everyone else knew too. They always told me so. Now, here was this guy telling me that I had some kind of condition. It was only when I made a supreme effort to teach myself to read that I began to make any progress at all.[1]

Work, training and education in prison are now mainly geared to prisoners acquiring skills that can be used on their release: a means of crime reduction or rehabilitation back into the community on their release. The system concentrates on basic education and wherever possible offers courses of instruction linked to various trades or careers. Naturally, there are those who are critical of this method and who would like to see a much broader approach to prisoner education. In *Chapter 9*, I mention some of the developments at my own local prison, Reading, by way of an example of what is being achieved by dedicated prison officers and tutors in some UK prisons.

I also try to get over how prison is a parallel universe where people's priorities and values undergo transformation. It also has its own hierarchy and internal economy. I remember that at Wandsworth the highlight of the week on A-wing was Thursday. Firstly, it was 'canteen day', which meant that we were able to visit the prison shop. This was a converted cell which housed what goodies inmates were allowed to buy with their allowances. Mine was fifteen shillings per week, the 'old money' equivalent of seventy-five pence, just enough to buy half an ounce of Boars' Head tobacco. Boars' Head was as black as tarmac and smelt much the same when lit. I could afford two packets of cigarette papers and one box of matches. Any money I had left over, I would save towards small luxuries such as a tube of toothpaste. Most of the products we were issued with were inferior to what could be bought in the canteen - in this case a foul tasting, gritty 'tooth powder'.

Secondly, Thursday was bath day. The bathhouse was situated near the exercise yard, so while we were walking around a dozen of us would

---

[1] I wrote about this in *I'm Still Standing*.

be hived off by staff and led there. We were given a clean shirt and a pair of socks and underwear - that had previously been worn by countless other inmates. The bath had just six inches of lukewarm water in it and - if I was lucky - I would have managed to hassle some shampoo. If not, I would have to wash my hair with the 'Old Windsor' soap supplied by the prison, which had its own unique aroma. Sometimes also Thursday was 'party night' in my cell. I felt marginally cleaner, had some tobacco to smoke and I was bursting with anticipation for the next enthralling episode of 'The Archers' at five minutes past seven.

I make a point of never complaining to an audience about these conditions. I deserved all that I got. I am sure most of my victims would feel that my sentences were too short and not tough enough. But I do point out how I used to feel very sorry for myself. When it comes to 'Question Time' people often ask me what it was that made me give up offending. It would need an entire book to explain this in detail, but there is also a short answer: it was when I stopped feeling sorry for *myself* and started to feel sorry for *my victims*. I know this is simplistic: but I came to the realisation that I was not really stealing inanimate objects but irreplaceable things 'with people attached to them' and in which they had invested time, energy and effort. Often those objects had an emotional attachment, whereas I stole simply to finance alcohol or drug addiction and all that mattered was the next fix or high. Getting my clients to appreciate the victim's perspective is an approach that I use when working with offenders today within a range of courses and programmes. An appreciation of the victim's position is also what underpins my interest in restorative justice. I say more about all of this in *Chapters 8* and *9*.

• • •

Burglary is a particularly nasty offence and it inevitably raises some pretty strong comments when I talk to an audience. I have to acknowledge that are always people who are less than forgiving about my past. There are cases where burglary has devastated people's lives by violating all that they hold sacred. It has driven some people to become prisoners in their own homes, too frightened to leave in case the perpetrator returns. Others are so traumatised that they feel they can no longer continue to live in the same house.

A good deal of this kind of debate now focuses on the right of an individual to defend their home. This flows from the case of the Norfolk farmer, Tony Martin, who received a rush of public sympathy when he was given a life sentence for shooting dead a sixteen-year-old burglar,

Fred Barras, and injuring his accomplice, Brendon Fearon, at Martin's remote farmhouse in Norfolk. The case captured the mood of the public. Martin's conviction for murder was later reduced to manslaughter by the Court of Appeal on the ground of diminished responsibility and the sentence to five years' imprisonment.[2] I have already noted in the *Prologue* to this work that there is every difference in the world between the use of reasonable force to defend the home and a punitive or revenge attack.

Martin became a kind of 'folk hero', which I think sums up the feelings many people have about being let down by politicians, the police and the courts, all of whom are seen as being soft on crime. Even people and organizations with liberally-inclined views seemed to come to the defence of Tony Martin. But his main sympathisers were the right-wing press, who argued for the right to shoot-to-kill when people are defending their homes, claiming that this was the thinking of a majority of the public. I doubt whether many of them would really have taken the drastic steps that Martin did, but around that time some people were feeling disenfranchised in the face of what they perceived to be an insurmountable wave of crime sweeping through the UK. So there was an outcry.

The murder squad headquarters in Norwich was inundated. One police officer was quoted as saying,

> It was like the American Embassy in Saigon just before they pulled out and left it to the Vietcong. Someone said we had better lease the helicopter again in case they start storming the building. They are blaming us for his conviction.

In 1999, Ann Widdecombe MP told the Tory party conference that the next Conservative Government would 'put the law in order' and that:

> Victims are not only those who suffer from crime but those who suffer from the law... I believe it is every citizen's right within reasonable and sensible limits to defend themselves, or their properties, against attack without then fearing a penalty at law. For too long, victims have been just another statistic. A great deal is said about the rights of the criminals rather than the rights of the victims.

---

[2] It was also revealed that Martin was suffering from Asperger's Syndrome which often causes people to seem eccentric or odd and become victims of teasing and bullying.

There were further outcries around this case all of which 'kept the pot boiling' and left me fielding numerous questions from various audiences: first, when Brendon Fearon, the surviving burglar, was given leave to sue Martin for the injuries he sustained on the night of the burglary. I am sure that the tabloids inflamed the situation. The whole fiasco petered out when Fearon did not proceed with his civil claim. Further outcries came when Tony Martin sold his own story to the press for a reputed £100,000, raising questions about whether convicted offenders should be permitted to benefit from their crimes; and finally when Fearon was paid a fee by the BBC to appear in a documentary about the case. But it was always the rights of householders that were to the fore. Ultimately, after great capital had been made by many people concerning the need for a change in the law, Home Secretary Charles Clarke decided that the existing law of self-defence and protection of property is perfectly workable as it stands.

• • •

I think people have been concerned about other turns of events. Lord Woolf, the Lord Chief Justice, remarked that courts should consider not sending certain burglars to prison at all - which sent the tabloids into a spin and further infuriated some people. But, as Baroness Helena Kennedy in her book *Just Law* (Chatto and Windus, 2004) states, both Downing Street and the Home Office immediately distanced themselves from this rather than lend support to the country's leading sentencing judge in his efforts to rein in the rush to imprison more and more people.

Lord Woolf was trying to make an important distinction. All of us who have experienced burglary know how violating the experience is but a break-in to your home while you are sleeping is very different from burglary of an empty office. I believe that we must judge each case on its own merits: if someone breaks into a house when the householder is at home then to my mind there is no doubt that the court should be considering a custodial sentence. But the term 'burglary' covers a multitude of sins - and the seriousness of an individual offence is nowhere near as cut and dried as the label 'burglary' implies. There are quite different levels of seriousness and - as I believe Lord Woolf intended to convey - there are a number of low-level burglary offences that can and have been successfully dealt with by means of community sentences. Economically, this makes sound sense: it costs a fraction of the public cost of incarceration, thus saving the taxpayer a great deal of money. What is more, this approach can be more effective in terms of crime prevention in the future if a proportion of offenders are persuaded to alter their ways through tried and tested community schemes, programmes and techniques. But the public and the media often have difficulty in understanding this. The desire to gain some kind of revenge is a strong instinct. How I see my role is trying to explain how negative some attitudes are if we really want people to stop offending.

• • •

'Dunce Visits Oxford', the headlines should perhaps have read when I was invited to the Oxford Union to take part in a debate on crime and punishment. This is where Prime Ministers and the cerebral *glitterati* of various other callings have been forged over the centuries - not just the Premier League of debating but solidly at the upper end. Here also it was that the child who had once been lost for words and afraid to answer back - or even to join in a conversation - came, many years later, to mix it with some of the most argumentative and thrusting high flyers of tomorrow. There is every difference in the world between hot air and physical violence and at the end of the day it is only because we have other ways of letting off steam that we are not carving each other up after the style of road rage, air rage or any other rage that you can mention. These learned debaters might dance around me with their abstract theories and silver tongues but when it came to the cut and thrust I was well away and there was no way that they could rile me. I completed my anger management course before most of those students started prep school!

CHAPTER 5
In the Media

CHAPTER 5

In the Media

A campaigner who bore a strong physical resemblance to the Nazi SS General Herman Goering confronted me in the Green Room. With his nose pressed flat up against mine the man told me in plain terms that I was wrong: people *should* be free to shoot burglars. I warned him that he was out of order and to 'back off'. It is one thing to encounter violence and intimidation in prison. They are perpetually in the air due to suspicion, mistrust, resentment or paranoia. It can be settling old scores or related to the kind of offence that someone has committed, especially against children. That is why vulnerable prisoners ask to go on 'Rule 43' as it is still called (when they ask for protection) - even though the number of the rule changed long ago! But you do not expect such aggression in the plush surroundings of a TV studio! I said that I was prepared for a rational discussion, but I would rather he did not act in such a confrontational way.

• • •

Whenever there is a high profile crime case these days, I find myself being contacted by the media for 'an ex-offender's view'. Events can sometimes escalate. One minute a striking soundbite can go out on local radio and the next minute the topic has reached the BBC World Service and the national press. At the height of the Tony Martin case which I mentioned in the previous chapter, I penned what I thought was an innocent little piece for my local rag, the *Reading Chronicle*. Under the headline 'No Place for Gun-law in a Civilised Society' I argued that we should not encourage the notion that ready violence is acceptable. It was just a 300-word article but it was picked up by 'stringers' for the nationals and led to a round of interviews with the press and both local and national radio and TV stations.

Later on, when Martin was refused parole, I was invited to appear on Richard Littlejohn's TV slot on Sky News opposite a representative of one of the groups seeking to free him. He was insistent that Martin should have been let out, despite the fact that he was still not taking responsibility for the death of the burglar he had shot and despite his lack of remorse. When it came to my turn, I said that I fully agreed with the probation officer's decision not to recommend release, adding that the whole chain of events showed a lack of victim empathy. There was no sign of any acceptance that using excessive force was wrong. I was buoyed by the fact that the Court of Appeal had turned down a legal move to overturn the Parole Board's decision indicating that there was still a risk of offences in the future. I went further, commenting that anyone who propounded views such as Martin's could be dangerous.

At this point the debate became heated. My opponent banged the table with his clenched fist so hard that it made the water pitcher and glasses wobble, sending splashes of water across the table. I said that with such an attitude there was small wonder people might get killed! This only enraged him further - and as I have already indicated his henchman was waiting for me outside!

• • •

Fortunately not every media debate ends like this. A few months later I was back on Sky. This time the subject was 'Offending Behaviour Programmes: Are They Working?' These are courses for offenders that aim to address their behaviour in subjects such as 'anger management', 'drink driving' or 'cognitive thinking'. Again Richard Littlejohn was the presenter and he reminded me about the earlier *contretemps*. He said that my opponent's attitude had not done himself or his cause any favours.

The Martin case meant that I was involved in a number of similar TV debates, including on one occasion with Tony Martin's solicitor on Independent Television News. John Suchet was the chairperson. The solicitor said that he believed Martin had acted in legitimate self-defence: the very argument that had been rejected both at his trial and when he appealed. I countered by suggesting that his actions had been fully premeditated. The solicitor tried to sidestep the issue, but Suchet pressed him, saying that the point I had made was important. Eventually we begged to differ - and there were no fisticuffs!

• • •

'Broadcasting House', I said as I jumped into a black cab on a hectic Monday morning. Weaving in and out of the traffic the cabbie cheekily asked, 'What's on today?' - and, without waiting for an answer and almost as if telepathic, added, 'You're not on that "Jeremy Vine Show", are you?' But the grilling really began after he learned that I was a probation officer and that Jeremy's programme would focus on 'Law and Order'. More assertions than questions: gratuitous advice about what to do with offenders!

I listened politely, keeping my own counsel, but allowing myself to give the occasional smile or non-committal grunt. There was no point in getting into an argument about whether sentences were tough enough or about the merits of Restorative Justice - and I was in no mood for a full-scale debate *before* the phone-in started!

'Hang the lot of 'em . . . and the do-gooders . . . Tell your friend Jeremy that!' If this cabbie were in charge I think that London would soon be 'The City of the Gallows' all over again - as it was in former times, with heads on spikes and bodies strung up from lampposts. I resolved to tell the next cabbie I met that I was a plumber and that my overalls were in my briefcase.

• • •

After a short wait in reception at Broadcasting House, a researcher for Radio Two came to collect me and take me to the studios in the basement. There I spent ten minutes chatting with the producer about my contribution: as a probation officer I could talk about crime prevention and as an ex-burglar I could offer advice on ways that listeners could try to protect their homes and belongings. It was also just days after Barry George had been convicted of the murder of the BBC TV 'Crimewatch' presenter Jill Dando. We should anticipate calls about the case.

I have appeared on a number of such programmes. They like to throw me to the wolves, wheel me out as 'cannon fodder'. I have learned that many people, especially victims of crime, feel cheated by the system and neglected. They feel removed from the level of attention and 'fairness' shown to offenders during their arrest, trial and sentence. Offenders and their families complain that sentences are too harsh: victims and their families complain they are too lenient. I mention more about what might be done to resolve this in *Chapter 8*.

The 'One O'clock News' was being read as I was led into the studio. I was greeted by the presenter, Jeremy Vine, and as the news faded out I put on my ear-phones and adjusted my tie. I have discovered that people do this sort of thing automatically even though they are on the radio and cannot be seen! I think they used to read the news wearing dinner suits, which is much the same thing. After a short introduction I fielded questions for forty-five minutes (which passed like forty-five seconds). I was getting used to answering listeners' questions on this type of programme. Neither was it the first time I had been involved with Jeremy, having been his guest on the Sunday morning programme, 'Broadcasting House' on Radio Four. I had learnt to do my homework and in this instance it led me to wonder about whether Barry George really was the killer. This was bound to bring controversy in its wake.

• • •

There was enormous sympathy for Jill Dando. Her murder shocked the nation, not least because she was so popular - 'the girl next door' - and greatly loved by her fans. She had appeared on TV so frequently that many viewers felt that they knew her like they know their next door neighbour. But there were others who were concerned about the jury's verdict. It was worrying that George had been convicted on circumstantial evidence. It would have been better to see the kind of closure that solid or 'hard' evidence produces.

I remember vividly the moment when I first heard that Jill Dando had been attacked. Reports were coming in over my car radio of the continued bombing on Serbian positions, which had lasted for over a month, in Kosovo during the war there. On the home front, there was fresh racial violence in the wake of bombings in Brixton following others in Brick Lane in London's East End. I was on my way to Huntercombe Young Offenders Institution near Henley-on-Thames to interview a young offender who was there on remand to await his sentence. Then there was a newsflash: Jill Dando had been involved in a mishap outside her home in Fulham. She had been injured and taken to hospital. Later in the day as I was driving home, the news broke that she had died of her injuries. By the time I arrived and turned on the TV the full, tragic story was emerging that she had been shot dead on her door-step. People had already started to lay flowers near her house.

This triggered a huge police investigation - in the full glare of the cameras. The information slowly seeped out that Jill Dando had been killed by a single shot to the head and by next morning there was a frenzy of speculation that this bore the hallmarks of a contract killing. Perhaps there was a link to something featured on 'Crimewatch', the programme she presented with Nick Ross, that looks mainly at unsolved crimes in conjunction with UK police forces and asks the public to help with information. The programme has been responsible for solving a number of major crimes and is supported by police forces across the UK. Could it have been that something she had said or done had run up against the Mafia or some other criminal cartel?

There were other theories: that it was a Serb revenge killing: because she had made a TV appeal concerning the Kosovo conflict - and had been targeted to show the British Government that Kosovans could strike anywhere; that the killing was the work of a former lover, distraught at her forthcoming marriage to the hospital specialist Alan Farthing; or that it was 'a nutter', someone who was obsessed with her as many people can become with media personalities.

The background to the case was also perplexing. With marriage in view, her house in Fulham was on the market. She would simply call in to collect the mail and check the place over. The times when she would do so were random and unpredictable. She did not even know herself when she was likely to go there. So how did the killer know that she would be there that morning? Or was the killer just an opportunist; or plain lucky that she turned up when she did?

• • •

Every aspect of the case became 'good copy', as newspaper editors say. Even the gun that was used became a topic in itself. Brian Cathcart's book *Jill Dando, Her Life and Death* (Penguin Books, 2001) reveals that police ballistic examinations showed that the cartridge found at the scene was made by Remington, USA for use with nine millimetre semi-automatic pistols: but it had various marks not consistent with standard manufacture. It was makeshift and had been put together in a primitive way.

In the underworld it is often the practice to collect the various components for a gun from different sources and to assemble these at home. Many such guns exist. Cathcart states that marks on the cartridge showed that it had been fired from a smooth bore weapon. Most gun barrels have 'rifling' to spin the bullet when fired and ensure greater range and accuracy. At some time the gun in the Dando case had been 'de-activated' by grinding down the barrel. But, again, such guns can be re-activated by amateur gunsmiths and though this may leave the gun without 'rifling' it may be adequate enough for criminal purposes.

Whether for these or similar reasons, people were 'sucked in' by the hitman theory. On one occasion I was in Nottingham appearing on a 'Kilroy-type' studio discussion programme on the same subject. After the show ended, I was collecting my things and about to grab a taxi when I was accosted by a robust, middle-aged woman with peroxide blonde hair, whose make-up looking as if it had been applied with a paintball gun! She came at me hammer and tongs, complaining that I was quite wrong for stating that I, personally, was against the idea that it had been a professional hitman. She was certain it was 'a hit'. When I asked how she knew, it turned out that her chief sources were red-top newspapers!

At this point in time I was being asked about the case so many times. If I was going to be 'in the media' I needed to know more about things first-hand and so I decided to spend a few hours visiting the area of the murder. Wearing my three-cornered hat - that of probation officer, ex-offender and self-styled 'sleuth' - I started to look again at the case.

A striking feature was that there was nothing on the face of things to indicate that Barry George was the kind of person who could carry out such a well-executed crime. Neither was there anything in his background to single him out as a particularly high risk offender. His 'bizarreness' - which I will describe - is really no different from that of hundreds of people whom probation officers deal with every day of the week! It is different only in terms of its specific nature - not its quality or strangeness. George was recognisable around his home area as 'an oddball'. But it is always difficult to predict accurately when 'oddballs' will turn into something worse. If we locked up everyone who stood out in a crowd we would need to double the number of prisons and even then they would be full to bursting point!

John McVicar, in his book, *Dead On Time* (Blake Publishing, 2002) gives a detailed profile of Barry George in which he describes his broken home, the fact that he was born with a cleft palate (which created more problems for him psychologically than being diagnosed in his teens with *petit mal* epilepsy: a form that involves attacks and possible alterations in consciousness), and that his father had been desperate for a son after his wife had given birth to two daughters. Correctional surgery remedied his palate, but George's upper lip was scarred and this left him with permanent speech difficulties. His father deserted the family for Australia when George was seven.

By this time, it was evident that George had serious behavioural problems. These resulted in him being admitted to a boarding school for maladjusted children. On leaving school at sixteen, George got a job as a messenger for the BBC at White City - a fixed term contract for six months - under the assumed name of Paul Gadd (which is the real name of the former pop singer, Gary Glitter). The job lasted just five months due to his bad timekeeping and 'confusion' when carrying out even routine tasks. He was bitterly disappointed that he did not get a permanent post because he was obsessed with stardom and, quite unrealistically, saw the job as a stepping-stone to celebrity. He did not work much after that. He was registered as disabled because of his epilepsy.

• • •

Barry George first came to the attention of the courts at the age of twenty when he pleaded guilty at Kingston Magistrates' Court to a charge of impersonating a police officer. The court received a psychiatric report but simply fined him five pounds. Outside court, he posed for pictures for the local newspaper. Still using the name, Paul Gadd, he boasted that he was related to a member of the prominent rock group, The Electric Light Orchestra.

Then, in 1980, he was prosecuted for two sexual assaults: approaching women he had followed and forcibly kissing them and fondling their breasts. He was convicted of one offence and acquitted of the other. Again, after seeing pre-sentence reports, the court sentenced him to three months imprisonment, suspended for two years so long as he did not commit another offence during that time. The following year, it was alleged that he raped a woman but he was not arrested until thirteen months after the offence. As part of a 'plea bargain' with the prosecutor, he acknowledged that he was 'guilty' of attempted rape and was given two and a half years' imprisonment to which were added the earlier three months from the suspended sentence.

Following, release from prison he befriended a journalist, Robert Charig. With his help George began to advertise himself as a stuntman in TV and films in his quest to achieve celebrity status - but this was short lived. He was involved in the Territorial Army at the time of the Falklands War. He tried to join a gun club but was turned down.

George then adopted a different alias and persona: Thomas Palmer, SAS hero. Around this time, he also became fascinated with the music of the rock band, Queen, and their lead singer, the late Freddie Mercury, who became his alter ego. He began to use the name, Barry Bulsara, thus employing Mercury's real surname. Mercury had a keen interest in Japanese culture. Barry George married Itsuko Toide, a Japanese woman but the marriage lasted only for a short time. She left him and returned to Japan because of his abusive behaviour.

Barry George lived in a flat at 2a Crookham Road, London (which is off the Fulham Road). I walked from there to Gowan Avenue where Jill Dando had lived. At a brisk pace it took me eight minutes. A younger person could possibly have shaved a couple of minutes off that.

• • •

So much for George himself. What of the investigation and the resulting controversy, so evident during the phone-in programmes that I took part in?

As the months passed after Jill Dando's murder, the police activity became less publicly visible than it had been at first but the media kept the story in the public eye. *The News of The World* ran a story that MI5 had been called into the investigation. *The Mirror* printed a story about a palm print found on the front gate of Dando's house. *The Mail on Sunday* demanded to know why the police had not interviewed a convicted rapist who worked for a security firm used by the BBC. *The People* led with a front page story that the security services had been tipped-off by Israeli intelligence that a senior figure in the Russian Mafia had ordered the killing because Dando rejected his advances when they met in Cyprus during one of her assignments.

The Sunday Mirror ran a front page story with the headline 'Jill's Killer Bought Gun in Pub'. Three men were said to have done so in a public house in the Midlands. Then *The News of The World'* printed another sensational headline, 'I Know Who Killed Dando'. This claim came from an underworld supergrass who had contacted the police saying that he knew the killer - and for money and an amnesty concerning his own crimes he would name that person. None of these stories had any truth or substance: but they are good examples of how the media tries to increase circulation and manipulate public opinion.

For the investigating team, the name 'Bulsara' (which as I have said had become George's alias) surfaced after a call was made to the incident room from Hammersmith and Fulham Action for Disability (HAFAD). The staff did not give the police the name 'Bulsara' at that stage, they merely said that someone had called in at eleven in the morning on the day of the murder who spoke about his health problems. He was in an agitated state. They told the man that he could only be seen by appointment and to come back the next day. He called in the day after that. No-one was sent to interview the HAFAD staff, so after two weeks they called again. This time they mentioned the name Barry Bulsara and said he resembled the E-fit picture of Dando's murderer that the police had released. More importantly, the police were this time told that he had arrived at HAFAD at 11.50 a.m. not, as previously stated, 11.00 a.m. - about twenty minutes *after* the murder. But the police had stronger leads; the call was logged and Bulsara marked down for interview. He remained in the queue for nine months.

When eventually interviewed, George told police that he was alone at home on the morning of the murder and went to HAFAD about 12.30. He could not be sure of the time. It was not enough to make him a suspect because he could provide an alibi. However, he was about the right age, height and build for the man described by witnesses. He gave a description of the clothes he was wearing and these were similar to the ones witnesses had said the gunman had been wearing. Then his background came to light, including his offences against women.

The police searched his flat. It was cluttered with boxes of old newspapers dating back a year and these obviously contained extensive coverage of the Dando murder. They took away dozens of rolls of undeveloped photographic film. When processed, these turned out to be clandestine pictures of women in the street. They did not find any firearms or ammunition, but did get part of a gun holster and an SAS-style knife. Other items pointed to the fact that George could have been obsessed by guns and women. But it was all circumstantial evidence. There were no forensic links to the murder. So they took away lots of clothes. Among these was a Cecil Gee three-quarter length coat similar to one that a witness had said the gunman had been wearing. After minute examination, this revealed a single spherical metallic particle in the lining of the left-hand pocket: the discharge residue from a firearm. It was one-hundredth of a millimetre in diameter and not visible to the naked eye. It contained three elements of the four metal elements from the shot that killed Dando. It was not conclusive.

Further forensic evidence came with the discovery of fibres consistent with the coat that Jill Dando was wearing when shot, which could have come from a pair of trousers taken from George's flat. But again this evidence was debateable and not conclusive. Five witnesses claimed to have seen George in Gowan Avenue on the morning of the murder. But there were conflicting descriptions of the gunman and just one positive identification.

George was arrested in May 2000 and charged with murder next day. In November there was a two-day committal hearing at Bow Street Magistrates' Court. The defence had recruited Michael Mansfield QC, well-known for his role in seeking to overturn miscarriages of justice. He had also acted for the Lawrence family at the public inquiry into the police investigation into the killing of the black teenager, Stephen Lawrence. He is very much 'in the media' himself.

I have bumped into Mike on other occasions, including at Oxford Crown Court at the retrial of Sara Thornton. She had been convicted of murdering her husband in 1989 by stabbing him to death as he lay on the sofa in a drunken stupor. She pleaded 'not guilty' on the grounds of provocation, a plea accepted by neither the prosecutor nor the jury, so she was sentenced to life imprisonment. Her first appeal was dismissed. Under intense pressure from women's groups her case was referred back to the Court of Appeal and in 1995 a retrial was ordered. In May 1996, she was convicted of manslaughter and sentenced to five years' imprisonment, but 'walked free' from court because she had already served the time.

Sara Thornton's retrial was another case that hit the headlines. I was involved in it as a probation officer because I was helping Joe Chapman, an ex-prison officer. Our job was to make sure that Sara Thornton had a safe house to go to each evening after spending the day in court. We kept her on the move, away from the press pack. That meant she went from one bed-and-breakfast establishment to another. We vetted the proprietors to make sure they were not taking a 'bung' from reporters and booked her in under assumed names.

I watched Mansfield in action: always impressive. I love the cut and thrust of the courtroom which can be sheer theatre sometimes. I should have done a law degree. I would have enjoyed being in there, mixing it with the best of them.

I also met Mansfield and his wife Yvette Vanson, the TV documentary maker, at a lavish legal function in Brixton. What sticks out in my mind is the food. What an indictment. Some of the finest legal brains in England were there and my main memory is that the food was great. Priorities!

During Barry George's committal hearing Mansfield tried to get the metal particle found in the Cecil Gee coat ruled inadmissible on the grounds that the coat was removed from the flat a fortnight before it was delivered to the laboratory for examination. In between times it was kept and transported along with other items from Hammersmith Police Station to be photographed at the police studio in Amelia Street, south London. The coat was taken from its sealed packet, placed on a tailor's dummy and photographed. Prior to this the police had been taking pictures of firearms. Despite Mansfield's powerful arguments the particle was ruled admissible.

• • •

Barry George's trial began before Mr Justice Gage and a jury in the Number One Court at The Old Bailey in February 2001. Before the jury was sworn-in there were four days of legal argument and then a seven week adjournment. But the judge did not lift reporting restrictions. There had been intense media interest but from the moment George was charged until the start of the trial nothing much was reported and no pictures of him were published at all. A legal challenge was mounted by the *Evening Standard* and the *Daily Mail* to revise the decision not to lift these restrictions at the start of the trial. Lawyers for the media successfully argued that it had started despite the fact that there had only been legal argument. The challenge was successful.

'First Picture: Man Police Say Shot Jill Dando'. Within hours the London *Evening Standard* was on sale complete with a mugshot of George. Next day his picture was on all the front pages. *The Mail* and the *Sun* went further by publishing a 'rogue's gallery' of pictures of George. The words 'weird' or 'oddball' were avoided but the inference was clear. Subliminal messages. Mansfield was beside himself. He claimed that the intense media interest made it impossible for his client to receive a fair trial: 'My client is being portrayed as a Walter Mitty character'. He argued that the jury could not fail to be prejudiced, saying that the case had an aura of 'guilt' around it. But the case went ahead. The judge later told the jury to put all the press coverage out of their minds and judge the case on the facts.

Leading for the prosecution was Orlando Pownall QC. Brian Cathcart (in his book mentioned earlier) describes George's behaviour in court by saying that 'he came and went . . . George did the sort of grimacing and blinking, the unsteady walking and heavy sighing that one might expect from a ten-year-old boy hoping to ham his way out of school'. And at the end of the trial, Mr Justice Gage remarked that after watching George's performance in the dock he was sceptical as to whether he was trying to manipulate the court. Five psychologists identified various conditions from which George was suffering, which included attention deficit hyperactivity disorder, somatisation, factitious disorder and histrionic narcissistic personality disorder. His IQ was 76 (the average being 100). They diagnosed him as being on the borderline of normal intellectual functioning; and his memory was very poor, as were his concentration and ability to plan and execute complicated actions. Along with his *petit mal* epilepsy, he had to have a mental health social worker sitting in the dock alongside him. A doctor was retained and seated in the well of the court to assess George as needed and his capacity to follow the proceedings. The court adjourned for ten minutes each hour so that he could be medically assessed.

The jury of seven women and five men took five days to weigh up the evidence before returning their verdict of 'guilty'. One of the female jurors had to withdraw because of a family bereavement: the jury returned a majority verdict of ten to one. Next day the media had a field day. George was labelled as a 'Sex Monster and Mad Assassin'. Readers might have believed that he had a string of rapes to his name. Not wanting to be outdone, the *Sun* carried the story that George was obsessed with Diana, Princess of Wales, and had also been planning to assassinate her - but instead had killed Jill Dando to whom his anger had been transferred.

• • •

A point I repeatedly made in media interviews was that the evidence was *thin*. It was circumstantial and to my mind inconclusive. Assumptions seemed to have been made based on George's oddball behaviour. The safeness of a conviction in such circumstances seemed as unlikely as John McVicar's obscure conclusion that George killed Dando as some kind of ritual sacrifice to the memory of Freddy Mercury.

From the medical evidence and his behaviour in court it was clear that George suffers from substantial learning difficulties. He would have been incapable of organizing a trip to the local supermarket, let alone carrying out a coolly executed murder in broad daylight on a London street and evading capture for a year. Neither the police nor the prosecution have ever discovered a reason - or 'motive' - to explain why George would have wished to shoot Jill Dando. No murder weapon was found. At no point did the supposedly less than intelligent Barry George make a mistake or give anything away to indicate his involvement. I am not sure that even the prosecution team believed that it would win.

Barry George appealed against his conviction a year or so later but that appeal was dismissed. Afterwards he issued the following statement:

> I did not murder Jill Dando and I believe that one day the truth will come out. I only hope and pray that this happens in my lifetime. I have spent over two years in prison for a crime I simply did not commit. I have struggled hard during this prosecution against me to keep my faith in the British criminal justice system. Today, that faith and belief has been destroyed.

He may have a point. Being 'in the media' can be a double-edged sword and the press can be either friend or foe depending on what sells newspapers. Even the news programmes have to be entertaining or we switch channels. To my mind there is something not right about the trial and conviction that I have described above - and the Dando case could well one day become another one in the growing UK catalogue of miscarriages of justice.

• • •

Of all the radio and TV presenters I have worked with, one of those who impressed me most was the late John Peel. On one occasion, Sue and I accepted an invitation to be interviewed by John for his Saturday morning Radio 4 programme 'Home Truths'. Normally, our children can be pretty blasé if when they hear their dad on the radio or see his picture in the papers. As they have got older and more independent they are only rarely interested in going along with me to wherever the programme or interview will take place. But when our then sixteen-year-old daughter, Sarah, found out it was John Peel who would be asking the questions she was not going to pass up the opportunity of meeting him. He was sixty at the time, which just goes to show how certain talents can attract listeners across the generations.

When we arrived at the studio we found John asleep with his feet on the table. He was wearing a pair of green Doc Martin boots, a T-shirt and jeans. The boots were what impressed Sarah the most. She was ushered into the control room whilst Sue and I sat at the table with John as he stirred himself back to life.

The topic was 'Relationships'. In our case the interest for listeners was how we came together: Sue from a middle-class background and privately educated; myself an ex-con with a record that would make the Artful Dodger look like a choirboy. Not only did we marry but now we have five children.

John was a skilled interviewer. He had a knack of putting people at ease and getting the best out of them. He made it seem like sitting by the fireside. The conversation just flowed and the time simply flew by in the half-an-hour or so that we sat there chatting. His voice was so familiar, having been heard on the radio for over thirty years and he had also done countless voice-overs for TV advertisements. At one point he asked me what finally caused my life to change.

A number of incidents flashed through my mind. There was the kindly Salvation Army lady who visited me in prison and who looked me in the eye and said that if I carried on the way I was going I would be lucky to survive beyond my thirtieth birthday. There was also a near transcendental and almost religious experience that I had one morning whilst I was in a rehabilitation centre when I woke up alone in my cell and saw what seemed to be a bright light shining in the distance. Then there was Sue. All of these things had played a part in causing me to build a new life or keeping me on the straight and narrow. But in the end I told him the single most compelling reason. 'It was when I stopped feeling sorry for myself and started to feel sorry for the people I had harmed'.

Here, the airwaves were being used as some kind of public confessional. I was being allowed to affirm before all and sundry both my relationship with Sue and all that held my life together. John was able to get through to people in that way. It was like talking to an old friend.

CHAPTER 6

Capital Punishment

CHAPTER 6

Capital Punishment

The conference room of Utah State Prison is situated at the foot of the mountains in Draper, USA. We were seated at a highly polished conference table there on which were plates of freshly baked croissants, muffins and Chelsea buns along with large jugs of freshly squeezed orange juice.

I was in Draper for a breakfast meeting with the warden of the prison, Hank Galetka, and his staff. He sat at the head of the table next to me flanked by his senior staff. Hank was a middle-aged, somewhat overweight, balding man, smartly dressed in a grey suit. As he sat down, his trousers rose above his ankles revealing that he was wearing cowboy boots. His stetson hat was on the coat stand, which left me in no doubt that I was in Cowboy Country.

• • •

I was in the USA to present a series of lectures on UK prison perspectives and had been invited to the prison to give a presentation at the Fred House Academy. The academy is situated outside the prison further up into the mountains. It is named after a police officer who was killed in the line of duty back in the 1980s and is in a picturesque setting with panoramic views of the mountains that surround the Utah Valley. It is a training establishment for prison staff and deputy sheriffs. They were keen to hear about my experiences in British prisons both as an inmate and as a probation officer.

As my talk was scheduled for later that afternoon, it gave me an opportunity to spend the morning shadowing Ray Wahi, the captain of the guard. Ray is a well-built man around six-and-a-half feet tall, with a shaven head and handlebar moustache. Like his colleagues, Ray was warm, friendly and accommodating but incredulous to hear that British probation officers do not carry guns.

'So how'dya get your customer to toe the line, Bob . . . How does law enforcement work with these community orders?', Ray enquired.

'I write them a letter . . . Give them a warning.'

'And if that fails . . .?'

'I write them another . . . with the warning underlined in red.'

'And next . . . You lock 'em up, Bob?'

'When I really mean business I underline the warning twice and mark the envelope "URGENT!"'

'You need to get yourself a revolver, Bob', he responded having twigged that I was exaggerating somewhat.

Firm enforcement of community orders is one key to their success, but the idea of probation officers riding into town toting a six gun made my mind boggle! It's easy to see how people can be made to feel small and inadequate. There's a great attraction in the idea of simply nuking problems but something more fundamental is needed for the long term. 'We work with the offenders . . . and often their victims . . . the idea is to build a "safe, just and tolerant society"'. Seeing that I was grasping at straws I rolled out the latest Home Office motto. Ray fixed me with the kind of perplexed look that was probably given to the Hebrew prophets.

Each time we passed someone they would say, 'Hi, Captain'. Compared with most UK prisons, Draper is large. It accommodates 4,300 prisoners, whereas Wandsworth Prison, one of the largest in England, has a capacity of just 1,440. They also have what Ray called 'a female facility' which we visited. The atmosphere reminded me of Holloway Prison in north London, where I visited from time to time.

Men and women prisoners each dressed from head to toe in white. White jackets, white trousers and white T-shirts - with the inmate's prison number across the right breast. In bold lettering on each prisoner's back ran the word 'INMATE'.

'Why are they dressed all in white, Ray?' I asked politely.

'So they will be easy to pick out when they escape'.

I guessed it was not my place to point out that the prison was surrounded by snow-capped mountains and that for several months of the year the valley below lay under a white blanket!

I was shown the workshop where the prisoners manufactured 'automobile' number plates. Then I was taken on a tour of the cellblocks. I was allowed to talk to the inmates at will. Some seemed to be doing pretty long sentences compared to the UK, often with the number of years to be served running well beyond the age that a human being could expect to achieve. But that number is usually chipped away by various appeal and parole processes so that the time actually served can be just a fraction of the sentenced time.

Whilst we were visiting the reception area, a vanload of prisoners arrived. It was like the opening scene from the feature film 'Shawshank

Redemption' as the men disembarked from the van. They were handcuffed and wore leg irons with another chain running from their wrists to their ankles. Then they were chained to one another at the waist. As they shuffled along in a line through rows of guards, I was plagued by the lack of hope in their faces. No matter what people have done, they should always be treated with dignity - but these prisoners were being treated like a herd of cattle: nameless, faceless people being rounded up by their rancher guards.

I asked Ray how they transported women prisoners, hoping that he would tell me that this was in a more dignified way. With signs of irritation on his face and the gaze that a mother cat has when she looks over her shoulder at kittens playing with her tail he answered, 'The same way we do with men prisoners'. To be fair, I suppose that one thing you can say about Draper Prison is that it cannot be accused of discrimination on the basis of gender. They treat folk in the same even handed, humiliating manner regardless of their sex!

• • •

As we approached the maximum security block one of the guards came hurriedly towards us.

'Captain!' said the guard, breathlessly, 'there are six in the maximum security block that will not go back in their cells'.

My mind started racing, wondering what Ray's reaction would be and for a moment I visualised the place as a smouldering ruin with the guards taken hostage. In the UK the prison staff would initially adopt a softly, softly approach. In the 1970s there was a TV comedy sit-com called 'Porridge' starring Ronnie Barker and Richard Beckinsale as two prisoners. Set in the fictional Slade Prison, one of the prison officers was a Mr Barraclough who was a kind-hearted officer with a gentle approach to the prisoners in his care. In the UK, officers would try to defuse any potentially riotous situation by sending in a Mr Barraclough-type officer, hoping that he could reason with the troublemakers. Only later would the MUFTI squad - or Maximum Use of Force Tactical Intervention squad - be sent for and full control and restraint techniques employed. Naïvely, I thought that Ray and his staff would respond to the uncooperative six men in much the same incremental way.

'TEARGAS 'EM!!!' ordered Ray. Sensing my shock, he turned to me and added, 'They sure as hell will go back to their cells now, Bob!'

A couple of guards put on gasmasks and went into the cell block firing canisters, which meant that all the prisoners in the block would be gassed whether involved in the protest or not. Ray quickly escorted me away from that block and took me to another part of the prison. There, in a dining room, a group of inmates were having lunch. We helped ourselves to a meal, then joined some them at one of the long tables.

I was desperate to talk about the teargas incident but neither Ray nor the prisoners seemed to have the slightest interest in discussing the matter apart from the odd, passing reference to it. I could only deduce from their lack of concern that it was a regular occurrence.

If I were an inspector of prisons I would certainly rate the food higher than the fare served in English prisons. More equivocally, there was an endless supply of free Coca-Cola from a machine, with the inmates free to drink just as much as they could manage without bursting, as and when they pleased. After lunch, Ray and I continued our tour. He took me outside into a compound. A helicopter hovered over the maximum-security block dispersing the remnants of teargas that still seeped out of the now deserted cellblock.

• • •

We walked across the compound to the perimeter fence, about twenty feet high with rolls of razor wire along its top. There was an observation tower overlooking the compound, from which a guard holding a high-powered rifle watched every move we made. Ray took out his personal radio and spoke to the guard informing him that I was a guest and he waved us on. As we approached the gate in the far corner, Ray again spoke to the guard telling him that we wished to go through it. The guard opened it electronically, we walked through and it closed behind us as we started to walk towards a building in the far distance. I asked Ray where we were headed and with his standard deadpan expression he answered, 'Death Row'.

Death Row was a two-storey building set apart from the rest of the prison. In the late-1970s this particular building became notorious, as I will explain shortly. Once inside, the ambience was quite different from that of the main prison. You could have heard a pin drop. The main part of Draper Prison had the continual din of inmates talking and iron gates and doors being slammed, keys being turned in locks. This place was different. It did not seem to have the normal humdrum of prison life.

We entered a room off the main cellblock. On the wall were photographs of the eleven condemned men being held there. Their names and dates of execution were printed below their pictures. Ray pointed out that the dates did not mean that much because most of the men had been on Death Row for some time and the dates kept moving forward with each round in the never-ending US appellate process. Some of the men had been on Death Row for ten years or more.

Ray told me that on average an execution took place every two years in Draper. In Utah State the traditional method of execution was the firing squad. But this changed shortly after my visit and they now use the modern and increasingly common method, 'lethal injection'.

Ray told me a story about a prisoner he was escorting to the execution chamber. They had strapped him in the chair when a call came through from the State Governor's office for a stay of execution while his last appeal was being heard. Ray then escorted the condemned man back his cell. Twenty-five minutes later there was another telephone call from the Governor's office saying that the appeal had been overturned so the order to execute the man should be put into effect. Ray then walked with the condemned man back to the execution chamber and said to him, 'You're a better man than me, I could not do this.' I felt like asking him whether the poor guy had any choice but bit my tongue. This was clearly a place where sensitivities were best kept to oneself.

We walked through the cellblock of Death Row. It was just after lunch so the prisoners were behind their doors, the silence piercing apart from the crackle of the guards' personal radios and their muffled voices. At the far end of the block was a door that led into the execution chamber. The chamber had no windows. There was a high-backed chair against one wall with straps attached to it, in which the condemned person was placed.

Firing squads were made up from volunteers: members of the public living in the area or areas were the crime or crimes took place. When volunteers were required, the prison authorities simply advertised for them in the local paper. I was told that there was never a shortage of willing hands. The volunteers remained anonymous. They were driven to the prison in a covered van and taken straight to the chamber where they were let in by a side door. They then took up their positions behind a canvas screen where each person was handed a Winchester rifle. One of these was loaded with a blank round so that the marksmen would never know who fired the four fatal shots. LaMar Eldredge, a former police officer with the Roosevelt Police Department in Utah, later explained to me that the recoil from a blank is nowhere near as forceful as that from a live round. But when firing at a *live* target, the adrenalin rush is so high that there is no sense of the recoil. 'Strange place, America', I was beginning to think!

A paper target was pinned over the heart and a black corduroy hood placed over the condemned person's head. About twenty feet away on the opposite wall was a canvas screen with five square holes in it, through which the firing squad would place their rifles. On one side of the room stood a row of twenty or so chairs for the witnesses, made up of the members of the press and authorities - together with any invited guests of the prisoner!

• • •

Draper Prison became a focus of world attention in 1976 after the US Supreme Court lifted its moratorium on the death penalty, put in place ten years earlier. That same year Gary Gilmore murdered two men. The first was garage attendant Max Jensen. Around 10.30 on a July evening, Gilmore walked into the Sinclair Service Station in Orem carrying a .22 Browning Automatic and ordered Jensen into the toilets and told him to lie on the floor with his hands under his body. Gilmore then put the gun close to Jensen's head saying, 'This one is for me.' He fired, pushed the gun against his victim's head again and added, 'This is for Nicole', firing once more.

When I visited the service station at roughly the same time of day that the murder was carried out I got a sense of what it was like on that fateful evening. As I parked on the forecourt with the temperature still in the seventies I could see Gilmore in my mind's eye walking across the forecourt and entering the kiosk. Then the two shots ringing out.

Next day Gilmore claimed his second victim, Ben Bushnell, manager of the City Centre Motel in Provo. Gilmore went to the motel where he told Bushnell that he wanted the cashbox and to lie on the floor. He then shot Bushnell in the head. Gilmore left the motel with the cashbox, which he emptied, then placed in a bush. He held the gun by the barrel and pushed it into the bush but the trigger snagged on a branch setting it off so that Gilmore was hit in the hand between the thumb and the palm. A witness heard the shot and spotted the trail of blood to Gilmore's truck, took down the number and passed it on to the police. Gilmore was later arrested and charged with the murders.

The City Centre Motel has not changed much since the time of the murder either. I sat in the car park, looking into the office and got a strong sense of what it must have been like. I pictured Gilmore quitting the office and making his way to his truck that he had parked on the other side of the highway and visualised him trying to hide the gun in the bushes. The area had an uncanny feel: like the location of the Bates Motel in Alfred Hitchcock's classic film, 'Psycho'.

Gilmore had been released the previous year on parole from a fifteen year sentence for robbery. At his trial, he told the court that he had chosen his victims at random and committed the offences to try to gain the attention of his estranged girlfriend, Nicole Baker - which he did in a perverted kind of way. He had problems with alcohol and drugs and a tendency to violent episodes. He was sentenced to death and ordered his lawyer not to appeal because he wanted to die. It would be the first execution on American soil since the moratorium.

The USA and the world were horrified when Gary Gilmore became an instant celebrity. I know that I followed the story with keen interest from my cell in Wandsworth Prison. Gilmore twice tried to commit suicide - to use the words of Oscar Wilde in his *The Ballad of Reading Gaol* so as 'to deprive the scaffold of its prey'. The situation became yet more sensational when Nicole Baker became involved in a suicide pact with him. She was put in a mental hospital and no longer allowed to visit him.

Before long, Gilmore's face was on the front covers of magazines, newspapers and being beamed out from TV sets around the world. His picture was printed on T-shirts and his uncle, Vern Damico, began to handle the mounting publicity. There was even talk of him being executed in one of the T-shirts and it being auctioned at Sotheby's!

Gilmore was executed at 8.07 a.m. on 17 January 1979. He invited Nicole Baker to witness the execution but her hospital would not let her to attend. Witnesses say that Gilmore appeared calm. It was widely reported that his last words were, 'Let's do it'. As he was shot, his head slumped forward into the strap, his right hand delicately lifted before it too dropped. The witnesses saw his blood flow from his heart down his shirt onto the floor. The prison doctor lifted the hood but reported he was still alive. Twenty seconds later he was dead. The execution was the first of some 800 across America since that time. His body was taken to the University of Utah Medical Centre where his organs were removed. Within hours, two people received his corneas thereby inspiring the Punk band, The Advert's, top twenty hit 'Gary Gilmore's Eyes'. 'Let's do it' has since been immortalised on every type of kitsch.

• • •

I talked with Bob Evens, now retired, but who had been a guard at the prison for twenty-three years, fourteen of those worked on Death Row. Bob was a quietly spoken, dignified man in his sixties. He was working there when Gilmore was executed and got to know him very well during the time he was in the condemned cell.

Bob told me that Gilmore was 'not just a double killer': his actions were more sinister. He had systemically executed his victims. Yet, even with this assessment of his charge, as time went by Bob was able to look beyond Gilmore's crimes and outer shell to a warm and sensitive human being with a keen sense of humour. Gilmore joked with the prison's medical officer about the donation of his organs. He had said that he wanted to leave his hair to Bob - for a transplant! He had also said, 'I don't suppose you will be able to use my heart, will you?'

He would also play practical jokes on the staff. Bob called them 'con jokes' - particularly when Gilmore would hide from the staff pretending that he had escaped. He was also a talented artist. Needless to say, the sketches he did whilst on Death Row are now quite sought after. Bob said he had 'an even temperament'. The only time he saw Gilmore upset was when there was a stay of execution. He would smash up his cell and complain: 'You said that you was going to kill me, now do it!'

At no time did Gilmore try to defend his actions. Never once did he try to shift the blame onto other people or onto the fact that he was addicted to drugs and alcohol. He took full responsibility. Interestingly, Bob went on to say that during all the time he had worked on Death Row, without exception, all condemned inmates had committed their offences while under the influence of alcohol, drugs or both. He read the Bible a great deal and believed in 'an eye for an eye and a tooth for a tooth'. One of his parting gifts to Bob was his personally autographed Bible. Clearly Bob was touched by Gilmore's attitude - and he described him as a 'real man'.

There was a lot speculation as to why Gilmore was so adamant about being executed. One theory was that a place in the history books beckoned - as the first person to face the death penalty in America in modern times. I questioned Bob about this but he dismissed it out of hand. He told me that in his view Gilmore was quite sincere in wanting to atone for the deaths of his victims with his own death and that this was his only motivation. Gilmore fervently believed that the only chance he stood of redemption was if he himself were to die.

Bob spent the last day and a half of Gilmore's life with him. He prepared his last meal of hamburger, hash browns, eggs, toast and coffee and he was with him when Father Meersman administered the Last Rites. He helped his colleagues to handcuff Gilmore and to put on the leg irons and saw him being taken to the execution chamber. He said that Gilmore was calm when they took him away. He said nothing. He just smiled at Bob. Once he was gone Bob recalls being physically sick. Gilmore was a human being whom he had come to know well and now they were going to kill him.

It was obvious from these conversations that Bob Evens has been deeply affected and emotionally scarred by Gilmore's execution. Even today he has flashbacks and wakes up in the middle of the night in hot and cold sweats. His gentleness and sensitivity were obvious throughout. Inexplicably, he remains a supporter of the death penalty.

• • •

What is the point of capital punishment? Many people might argue that it is a deterrent but the data suggest that it has precious little real value in preventing people from committing serious offences. At one extreme, terrorists would line up to be executed to further their causes and achieve martyrdom whilst at the other extreme nothing, it seems, will ever curb the true crime of passion.

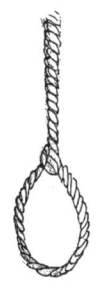

In the final analysis capital punishment is a tool that can be used in the name of justice so that society can reap revenge and retribution. But it achieves little beyond vengeance. In addition, an innocent person may be wrongly convicted of offences that in the old days would have attracted the death penalty - as in a long line of modern miscarriage of justice cases in the UK, starting with the Guildford Four, the Maguire Seven and the Birmingham Six in the 1970s.

• • •

One of the most telling indictments of capital punishment in the UK and a case that left me with nightmares at the time is that of Derek Bentley who was hanged in Wandsworth Prison in 1953 for the murder of a police officer. I remember witnessing the public outrage that engulfed the case due to the fact that most people believed Bentley to be innocent. There was also concern about a lack of true justice in that Christopher Craig, Bentley's co-accused who was a juvenile and who fired the fatal shot, was too young to be executed. The events were a talking point for months in the neighbourhood and at school. They were both local lads. I remember that on the day of the execution you could touch the gloom. But we were civilised people so there was a minute's silence before lessons started.

A few years later I could easily have been either of those young men. There were many parallels in particular between Derek Bentley's life and mine quite apart from the fact that we came from the same part of south London. The authorities had labelled us both 'educationally subnormal'. Due to my lack of prowess I was easy prey to the bad elements of society and vulnerable to peer pressure and befriending younger kids. Since school had become so stressful I would skive-off at the least opportunity even if this meant inventing imaginary illnesses and similar excuses. Truants are always at risk of descending into crime proper.

John Parris, who was leading defence counsel for Christopher Craig, gives a detailed account in his book *Scapegoat* (Duckworth 1991) of Bentley's background. He was born, one of twins, in 1933. The other twin, delivered later, died within two hours. At the age of four years, he fell off a lorry, which triggered an epileptic fit following which minor fits became a regular occurrence. From 1941 to 1943 he attended Camrose Avenue School, Islington. Twice the family home was destroyed in air raids and on the second occasion he was buried in debris and had to be pulled out by rescue workers. At the age of eleven he went to the John Ruskin School in Walworth and it was there that it was discovered that he was still illiterate. In 1945, the family moved to south London and he went to Norbury Manor School where he met Christopher Craig.

Since Bentley was frequently truanting, he was brought before the magistrates where an attendance order was made and he was transferred to another secondary school, Imgrams, for four months before being transferred back to Norbury Manor. The deputy headmaster told reporters that the school was lucky if he attended once a week. He also described him as 'like a great lump of lard, an utterly worthless piece of humanity.' I remember similar sentiments being thrown in my direction. It gets to you very quickly. We probably read the same comics and revelled in the exploits of Desperate Dan or Tom Mix.

In 1949, Bentley appeared with another boy at Croydon Juvenile Court[1] and was found guilty of two offences: attempting to break-and-enter and attempting to steal ten shillings and a quantity of bus tickets. He was bound over for two years and another school attendance order made back to Imgrams. It was the ninth time he had been shuttled backwards and forwards between schools. The following summer he reached the legal school leaving age and that was it as far as his meagre education was concerned. Like I did, he left school for good the moment the time came.

It was not long before he was in trouble again. This time it was for stealing tools from a building site. He was sent to an approved school in Bristol where tests showed that he had an IQ of 66 (the average being 100) and he was classed as 'feeble-minded'. On his release he went home

---

[1] The juvenile court became the youth court in 1991.

to live with his parents, his older sister Iris, who adored him, and his younger brother, Denis. He was so traumatised by the experience of being away from home that he did not set foot outside his house for the best part of a year afterwards.

• • •

I remember that when I was 15 years old I had, like Derek Bentley, become vulnerable to the kind of peer group pressure that calls for a demonstration of one's nerve and mettle. Two friends from school had stolen a motor scooter and one of them offered to take me for a joyride. I went along with the plan like a three year old who had just been offered a bag of sweets. This was the way to make my mark, become one of the gang. They might be into offending but at least they acknowledged my existence, whereas nobody else seemed to do so. We had not travelled far when we were stopped by the police and arrested.

The three of us appeared in the juvenile court. My two co-defendants, who had actually stolen the scooter, were both fined and like me, received a driving ban. We were puzzled by this because none of us was old enough to drive! They looked at our school reports. My co-defendants had glowing testimonials but mine was predictable in its use of derogatory language. My headteacher and my family just went along with what every school I had attended said of me - in effect that I was useless, a lost cause. I in turn believed this image that other people had painted, which led me to follow self-destructive habits, behaviour and routines. It took nearly thirty years before I overcame the deep-rooted problems that it created. Bentley was never to get a second chance.

My school reports also said that I was 'a disruptive influence' in school which I know was not true. I found it difficult to concentrate in class because I did not understand what was going on. The worst that can be said of me that in an attempt to gain some peer approval and make up for lack of academic prowess, I became very easily led by the other boys to do things that would wind up the teachers. And so with the scooter. I was charged with theft even though I was only 'being carried' on it, a somewhat lesser offence. For some reason the magistrates singled me out as the ringleader and I was given a two-year probation order.

A year into that order I was out one evening drinking with about fifteen other youths and I got very drunk. I have a vague memory of a horrendous fight breaking out, which led to windows being smashed and tables and chairs being thrown across the room. It was like a bar-room scene from a Wild West movie and that is how it seemed at the time. Unreal. As if I were watching it on a big screen. I was at the back of the room when the fighting was going on and too drunk to do anything sensible. I recall being hit by a missile and that was it. By the time the police turned up there were only myself and two other people in the place. I was nursing a head wound, but being drunk I was not able to make my getaway like the more streetwise ones did. I was arrested and charged with affray. By then everyone was working on the principle that as I was there I must be the cause of the disturbance - when in fact the only real crime that I had committed was being there and being drunk.

What I think I am trying to say is that if you are 'not that bright' - or have begun to think of yourself in that way - and have a poor self-image and a need to impress, become a 'people pleaser', then it is easy to find yourself on the wrong side of the law - and events can so easily escalate. In a way I was engulfed by crime and events around me rather than being someone who *embraced* it. I dread to think what I would have done if someone had stuck a gun in my hand.

• • •

At the age of nineteen, Bentley rekindled his friendship with Christopher Craig who was by then a fresh faced sixteen-year-old, a local tearaway with an obsession for guns. Craig introduced Bentley to some of his friends who were involved in petty crime. Bentley was attracted to their lifestyle. He admired, in particular, Craig's elder brother Niven who was well-dressed, drove a Buick convertible and was always in the company of attractive women. At that time, there was still rationing on food, tobacco and other goods, but Niven always had cigarettes and nylon stockings to sell on the black market.

Bentley became a 'people pleaser'. He would do virtually anything to gain approval. On one occasion he stole the keys from a local butcher's shop just to impress Craig and the others.

In 1952, Niven was sentenced at the Old Bailey to twelve years' imprisonment for robbery. Christopher Craig and his parents were in court to hear the sentence pronounced. Craig was taken aback by this and was consumed with hatred for the police. He blamed them for his brother being in jail. Two days afterwards, Bentley, Craig and three others set out to break into the butcher's shop. Bentley had with him a knife and on the way Craig produced a knuckleduster and gave it to Bentley as a present. When they arrived, the butcher was stocktaking. The other three members of the gang left to go the cinema but Bentley and Craig wandered around the streets. They walked along Tamworth Road in the direction of West Croydon until they got to Barlow and Parker's Wholesale Confectioners.

Craig suggested that they break into the premises. He was the first to climb the gates, followed by Bentley. They scaled the drainpipe to the roof but unbeknown to them, Mrs Ware and her husband, who lived next to the warehouse, had seen them and called the police. Meanwhile, on the roof, Bentley was trying to open the door to the stair head with his knife. It was at this point that Craig produced a handgun.

The first police officer on the scene was Detective Constable Fairfax, who climbed onto the roof and grabbed Bentley. He had him pinned against the wall. Bentley told DC Fairfax that Craig had a gun. Fairfax walked toward Craig telling him to hand it over and to surrender. At this point Bentley called to Craig, 'Let him have it, Chris'. Shortly after that Craig fired the gun at the floor, and the bullet ricocheted hitting Fairfax in his left shoulder. The wound was relatively superficial and the bullet did not penetrate the skin. Craig continued to fire at random.

Police Constable Miles gained entry to the roof through the door in the stair head. As he walked onto the roof he was shot between the eyes and killed instantly. Bentley was taken off the roof by armed police who had arrived at the scene. Being cornered, Craig jumped off the roof. His fall was broken by a greenhouse, nevertheless he suffered severe injuries, fracturing his breastbone, spine and left wrist.

Next day the *Daily Mail* front page headline ran, 'Chicago Gun Battle in London: Gangsters with Machine Guns on Roof Kill Detective, Wound Another'. The article read, 'The London crime wave reached a new peak last night. A detective was shot dead and another seriously wounded in the second battle of Sidney Street'.

Bentley's barrister, John Parris, interviewed Craig in Brixton Prison and stated that Craig had told him that while Bentley and Detective Constable Fairfax were hiding behind one of the stair heads Fairfax had sent Bentley out to get the gun from him. Craig had told Bentley to back off or he would shoot him as well. Craig went on to say, 'One of most terrible things that happened was that Bentley was turning against me. He was helping the police and they got him to try and persuade me to give myself up'.

Clearly, this piece of evidence was of crucial importance for the defence of Bentley but damning to Craig's defence that he had been firing into the ground or up into the air in order to frighten off the police and that the death of PC Miles was an accident. This new admission would have been be totally destructive to Craig's defence, since it showed that he was willing to kill or injure even his own friend.

Parris went to a joint conference with Bentley's counsel, Frank Cassels, to take the information that Craig had given him about Bentley trying to persuade him to give himself up. Parris was somewhat taken aback with Cassels's opening words, 'I think both the little bastards ought to swing'. His personal view was that anybody who carried a gun and killed a police officer should hang for it. Many commentators believe that Cassels was influenced by his personal feelings. However, if counsel were only to represent those with whom they sympathised a great many defendants would go unrepresented!

During the 1990s there were poll tax riots in London. I am sure there were many police officers who did not agree with that tax but they had to uphold the law by policing the riots. It was same for Frank Cassels. Even though there was no great empathy, he did contrive to make sure that his client got the best defence possible, limited as it was by the evidence and resources available to him. Nevertheless, he has been criticised for the way in which he conducted Bentley's defence. Much of that criticism was unfair.

In those days there was no legal aid, only the Poor Prisoner's Defence scheme, under which a pittance would be provided by the state and not enough, for example, to instruct independent consultants to write reports on Bentley's state of mind or interview expert witnesses. There were no highly organized campaigning groups or academic departments specialising in death penalty issues to come forward with support - as there are now. With hindsight it is difficult to see how there was time to mount a *proper* defence. The Croydon magistrates committed the case for trial at The Old Bailey within days. Just five weeks later, both Craig and Bentley were convicted of murder.

• • •

Frank Cassels later became a judge and his path was destined to cross with mine, as well as Bentley's. He was thought of by the criminal fraternity as 'firm but fair'. I appeared in front of him in the 1970s at Kingston Crown Court where I was acquitted of burglary (of which, I should stress, I was innocent) but found guilty of assaulting a police officer whilst resisting arrest (of which I was guilty). He sentenced me to six months' imprisonment. The following year I was put up in front of him again. This time I was sentenced to two years for another burglary. I had been caught 'bang to rights' coming out of a big house in Purley, Surrey, with my arms full of swag. I thought that he dealt with me fairly on both occasions.

The Craig and Bentley trial was initially listed before the Lord Chief Justice, Lord Goddard for 4 December 1952. John Parris had only received the brief to defend Craig on December 2 and he met with Lord Goddard to request an adjournment to allow him more time to prepare. Lord Goddard was positively hostile to the application, stating that any delay would greatly inconvenience him. He told Parris that he thought Craig would surely plead guilty to murder and that he could see no grounds for a manslaughter verdict. Parris states in his book that he wrestled with Goddard to secure an adjournment but felt Goddard was 'hell bent' on murder convictions for both defendants at all costs. In the end, after Parris had applied enormous pressure, Goddard relented and agreed to an adjournment for five days.[2]

The atmosphere in Number One Court at The Old Bailey - now part of the Crown Court in Inner London - is daunting even when the courtroom is empty. I have been there a number of times either as the defendant or as a probation officer! It is a great Edwardian room with creaking oak panels and spotless white plasterwork above. The judge's bench runs across its width at one end. Looking down upon the barristers is the jury box. In the well of the court sit the clerk and the usher, while perched high to the left, above the clock, is the public gallery which seats about thirty people. Directly opposite the bench,

---

[2] Parris goes on to say that he believed Goddard was a sexual pervert who would have an orgasm whenever he sentenced a young man to death. He states that he had numerous conversations with Goddard's clerk, Arthur Smith, who told him that he kept a spare pair of trousers in Goddard's chambers for this eventuality.

across the well of the court, nowadays surrounded on three sides with protective glass, is the dock, big enough for a dozen defendants and with large leather seats. Behind the dock is a narrow, white tiled staircase that leads to the cells below.

Bentley and Craig were brought up from those cells. Beginning with Craig, each was asked whether they were guilty of murdering Police Constable Miles. Both entered pleas of 'not guilty'. The all male jury was then sworn in. Christmas Humphreys QC was leading for the prosecution which carried the burden of proving to the jury beyond reasonable doubt that Bentley and Craig had, expressly or implicitly, agreed to use such violence as was necessary to evade capture. The mere possession of weapons by both men raised a *prima facie* presumption of such a prior agreement.

Although Craig had fired the shots and at the time of the shooting Bentley was technically already under arrest, it was argued by the prosecution that Bentley incited Craig to begin shooting by use of the words, 'Let him have it'. This would make Bentley equally responsible for the wounding of DC Fairfax and the murder of PC Miles.

No medical evidence was put forward to show that Bentley had a mental age of eleven. The main prosecution witnesses were three policemen who had been at the scene: DC Fairfax, PC McDonald and PC Harrison. Reading the miscarriage of justice papers of July 1998, it occurred to me that the witness accounts of those events were almost identical, word-for-word. Supporters of Bentley have often argued that this shows that the evidence was manufactured - in other words that the police lied at the trial. Nowadays, statements that match word-for-word call for an explanation at least and they may be evidence of fabrication.

Bentley and Craig were each found guilty. The jury recommended mercy for Bentley but, whatever might happen later, when Goddard passed sentence there was only one sentence that he could order. The black cap was placed on his head and he turned to Bentley and said:

> Derek William Bentley, you are 19 years of age. It is my duty to pass upon you the only sentence which the law can pass for a crime of wilful murder. The sentence of this court upon you, is that you be taken from this place to a lawful prison and thence to a place of execution and there you suffer death by hanging; and that your body be buried within the precincts of the prison in which you shall have been last confined before your execution and may the Lord have mercy on your soul. Take him down.

The black cap was removed and Goddard turned to Craig:

Christopher Craig, you are under age but in my judgment and evidently in the judgment of the jury you are the guiltier of the two. Your heart is filled with hate and you murdered a policemen without thought of his wife, his family, or himself; and never once have you expressed a word of sorrow for what you have done. I shall tell the Secretary of State when forwarding the recommendations of the jury in Bentley's case that in my opinion you are one of the most dangerous young criminals who has ever stood in the dock. I shall recommend the time which I suggest to the Secretary of State that you shall be kept in confinement. The sentence upon you is that you be kept in strict custody until the pleasure of Her Majesty be known. Take him down.

• • •

Derek Bentley was taken to Wandsworth Prison, which is just a few miles from his home in Norbury. The condemned cell was on E-wing on the second landing (E2). It was a double cell fifteen feet wide by fourteen feet long, decorated in brown and green paint divided by a black border running round the wall at chest height. The furnishings were sparse consisting of a bed, table and three chairs. There would have been a wardrobe on castors pushed up against the wall. The purpose of the wardrobe was to conceal a door that opened straight onto the execution chamber. The wooden scaffold was immediately behind the wall and the 'trap', through which he would be plunged with the rope around his neck, was no more than twelve feet from where Bentley would have slept. On the other side of the cell were a bath and a toilet. The cell had a connecting door into another room with a glass partition where Bentley would have received visits from his family, friends and legal representatives.

I have been an inmate at Wandsworth and was frequently housed on that same landing. I have walked past the condemned cell on the way to the exercise yard and as I stalked around the yard I often wondered what a condemned prisoner would have been thinking. What must have been going through their minds remains hard to contemplate. How the authorities could act in that way seemed barbaric.

When capital punishment was abolished in the UK in 1965, the 'topping shed', as the condemned cell and scaffold were known, remained empty until the early 1970s when the gallows was dismantled and sent to join similar artefacts in the Prison Service Museum at Newbold Revel near Rugby. It was designed so that three prisoners could be executed simultaneously. As far as I have been able to find out there never was a triple execution, but there were double ones. The gallows beam remains in place at Wandsworth to this day, but the condemned cell is now the prison officers' tearoom and the old execution chamber now used for training them in control and restraint techniques.

Bentley was in the condemned cell for just over six weeks. During that time there was a loud chorus of disapproval from the public, with people lobbying their MPs and Bentley's family gathering a huge petition with thousands of signatures. On January 13 1953, Derek Bentley's appeal against his murder conviction was dismissed. All prisoners awaiting execution had two prison officers with them twenty-four hours a day in three shifts, the last shift coming on a few minutes before the execution to avoid a personal relationship with the prisoner developing. They were hand picked officers, known as the 'Death Watch'. It must have been emotionally damaging for them.

• • •

Late on the afternoon of January 27, as was the custom, Albert Pierrepoint, the public executioner, and his assistant arrived at the prison to prepare for the execution that was scheduled to take place the following day. They were greeted with jeers from the crowd that had gathered outside. Later that evening, Bentley received his final visit from his parents and sister, Iris. As was the convention, Pierrepoint spent the night in the prison and at some point would have viewed Bentley through a spy hole in the door of his cell, to assess his height and weight for the purpose of getting 'the drop' right. Whilst Bentley was out of the cell the gallows would have been tested, using a sandbag that was also left on the rope overnight to eliminate any 'stretch' in it.

Around seven o'clock next morning, Pierrepoint would have re-set the trapdoors in the execution chamber and made his final adjustments. He then coiled the rope and secured it with a piece of thread so that the noose dangled at chest level to prevent Bentley falling over it. About the same time Bentley was given his own clothes to wear and attended by a priest and the prison doctor. Just before the appointed time the execution team formed outside the condemned cell and on a signal from the Governor, the wardrobe was pushed to one side and the door to the execution chamber flung open. With the command, 'Stand up!' from the chief officer as he entered the cell, Bentley was passed handed some brandy and told to drink it quickly. Pierrepoint and his assistant would by now have taken total charge of the proceedings.

Bentley had his arms pushed behind his back and the assistant secured his hands with a leather strap. Pierrepoint stepped in front of Bentley, loosened his collar, looked him in the eyes and said, 'Follow me, lad, it will be all right'. With that, Pierrepoint turned and walked into the chamber. Two prison officers grabbed Bentley by the arms and walked him into the chamber. They led him onto the trap door, which had a 'T' chalked on it on which to position the condemned man's feet, exactly over the middle of the trap. In case Bentley fainted at the last moment, he was supported by two prison officers.

Pierrepoint placed a white cotton hood over Bentley's head and positioned the noose round his neck whilst the assistant strapped his ankles. The noose was adjusted so that the eyelet was tight under the angle of the left jaw. When all was ready, Pierrepoint removed the safety pin from the base of the operating lever and pushed it to release the trapdoors. Bentley dropped through the trap and hung motionless in the cell below, unconscious and with his neck broken. The whole process took somewhere under twenty seconds.

An hour later, after death had been certified by the prison doctor, notice of execution was posted for the benefit of the public on the main gate of the prison. Outside, the crowd had swollen to several hundred protesters. One wonders what that number might have been today. Inside, inmates had taken their cue from the people outside and started to bang on their doors with their tin mugs, and the whole prison went into total lockdown for three days. This meant that prisoners were only let out of their cells in small numbers, to prevent trouble. Later that day Bentley's body was buried behind the small exercise yard on E wing. Each year on January 28, for the next forty-four years, Iris Bentley would lay flowers at the gates of Wandsworth Prison until her own death in 1997.

• • •

It is astonishing to me that Bentley was convicted of murder in the first place but further that he did not receive the prerogative of mercy, which I think is what everyone expected. But what really beggars belief is that it was not until forty-six years later that he was given a posthumous pardon. What must his family had gone through over those years? His parents campaigned until their deaths in the 1970s and Iris Bentley continued the fight until 1997.

I think that amongst the establishment from Lord Goddard downwards there was a feeling that following the death of a policeman the public interest demanded a sacrifice and a scapegoat. It has often been said that the period shortly after World War II was a lawless one and Bentley probably suffered the consequences of that perception. Craig was released from prison in 1964 and has led a law-abiding life ever since. Derek Bentley would probably by now have been a grandfather, like me, but in his seventies.

• • •

There are other questionable cases from that era but I cannot go into detail about them here. They eventually led to the death penalty being abolished after a lifelong campaign by Sydney Silverman MP who, though he saw it suspended in 1965, did not live to see it finally abolished in 1969 under the Labour Home Secretaryship of the late Lord Callaghan. The cases include that of Ruth Ellis, the last woman to hang in Britain, in 1953. Nowadays, there is concern at the number of convictions being declared 'unsafe' by the Court of Appeal, particularly for serious offences such as murder and terrorism. Yet surveys show a worrying level of support for capital punishment to be reinstated - equally among both young and old. In recent years, the issue has become entwined with cases like the Soham murders of the ten-year-old girls, Holly Wells and Jessica Chapman in 2002 or the fear of a terrorist attack to rival September 11, 2001 in the USA.

But since the UK ratified the Sixth Protocol to the European Convention On Human Rights in 2000, capital punishment cannot be restored - at least not so long as the UK remains within the EU. The protocol also prevents the extradition or deportation of people to foreign climes if they might then face the death penalty there.

We tend to judge a community by the way its treats its weaker citizens, including those who break the law. Britain, in common with most other developed nations, has to all intents and purposes consigned the death penalty to the history books. But people of a passionate disposition - or who fear some dreadful chain of events that could lead them to the condemned cell, as I did in my shady past - should avoid places like China, Russia, Saudi Arabia or Nigeria - and of course the home of gunslinging probation officers, the USA!

CHAPTER 7
The Great Train Robbery

Chapter 7

The Great Train Robbery

There is a story about the Devil who poses the following question to one of his potential converts: 'Would you tell a lie for a million pounds?'
'Yes, of course I would', answers the person, without hesitation. Then the Devil asks a further question:
'Would you tell a lie for tuppence?'
'Of course I wouldn't, what sort of person do you take me for?!'
The Devil then adds, 'Now we have established what sort of person you are, all we have to do is settle the price!'

Many people say that it is the same with crime: 'Every man has his price'. The idea that people can be bought 'if the price is right' - by money or whatever - is part of the bedrock of popular culture. It can serve as an excuse for the petty offender who sees it as justification for his or her lesser transgressions. It explains a good deal of corruption. Occasionally, the offenders justify their activities to themselves by the sheer scale of what is involved and the issue may seize the public's attention because the offence really is 'The Big One'.

• • •

I walked into the Groucho Club in Dean Street in the heart of London's West End. It was a lovely warm August day: not really one to be indoors but I was there for a luncheon appointment. I had arrived a few minutes early, so I sat at the bar and ordered a sparkling mineral water with lots of ice and lemon. As I wandered over to an empty table, I noticed several showbiz people: faces I recognised from TV and films. They were evidently living a more sumptuous lifestyle than I was! 'This place is full of "luvvies"', I thought to myself.

I was starting to feel out of place when I glanced over to the door and noticed that my host had arrived. He was Paul Ashton the film producer. We shook hands. I had known Paul, who is in his early forties, for a year or more. He had shown an interest in making a film based on my life story and I had signed an option with his company. He was smartly dressed in a blue suit, his shirt open at the collar. We were trying to coax Sir Anthony Hopkins - Tony Hopkins - to play a role in the film. I had worked with Tony on a promotional video for a charity in the 1990s. We were both recovering alcoholics who had drifted into the same meeting of Alcoholics Anonymous one day in London.

Tony had since taken up residence in California and it was proving difficult to communicate with him but we knew that if we could link his name with the project there would be no difficulty getting financial backing. Paul and I had been willing to fly out to Hollywood to discuss the idea first-hand, but I had received a message saying that Tony had given our proposal close consideration but could not take the part. He explained that he was disillusioned with the British film industry and did not want to work in the UK again - at least for the time being. He said ours was a worthwhile project and wished us every success. Paul consoled me by saying that it often takes years from the time a movie is conceived to the first day of filming.

But we were not at the Groucho Club to discuss my film. As we sat chatting the next guest arrived. He was Bruce Reynolds, the Great Train Robber. He is a tall, slim man, now in his seventies with snow white hair. He was wearing gold-rimmed spectacles and a light, stone-coloured summer suit with a white shirt and blue tie. Unlike me, he seemed completely at home. He would be at home anywhere: whether in Wandsworth Prison or the lounge of the Ritz Hotel! Forty years earlier, in 1963, Bruce Reynolds led a gang of fifteen men in one of the most notorious crimes in British criminal history. The media dubbed it 'The Crime of the Century' and I can still see the headlines. I was living in south London at the time and remember people chattering about it in the pubs and clubs, trying to figure out who was involved. Those of us in the criminal fraternity tried to remember who had been missing from 'our manor' and the regular watering holes. Who did we know who could pull off such a stunt? Was anyone spending money all of a sudden? The underworld was ablaze with rumour and speculation.

A knock on effect of the robbery was that daily life became difficult for 'ordinary criminals' like myself. It became harder to place ill-gotten gains, because outlets were being turned over by the police left, right and centre as they looked for anyone or anything that might lead them to the perpetrators. At the same time, every excuse was used to hassle people. I tried touting my spoils around the local pubs but that was risky. A couple of acquaintances had been arrested trying to sell the proceeds of a burglary to a couple of undercover police officers! If ever you had been able to trust anyone in gangland, you certainly could not trust anyone now. Everywhere you went there were police officers or people ready to grass to save their own skin.

The Great Train Robbery remains the benchmark by which largescale property crimes - 'acquisitive crimes' as they are sometimes known - fall to be judged. It still figures in the newspapers whenever there is a major heist. When Bruce and his south London gang held up the Glasgow-to-London mail train their £2.6 million pounds haul in used banknotes was a huge sum, around £40 million by today's standards and thus in a similar league to the Brinks Matt gold bullion robbery, the unsuccessful attempt to steal the Millennium diamond and the raid on the Northern Bank in Belfast. Even today the names of the gang trip off the tongue of many people of my generation: Ronnie Biggs, Charlie Wilson, Roy James, Gordon Goody and Buster Edwards. Some were given thirty year sentences. The events were so out of the ordinary that, at the time, many people seemed to be saying 'Good luck to them' - almost in the tradition of Robin Hood, Dick Turpin, Jack Sheppard and Jonathan Wild, the inventor of organized crime. But the shine went off the gingerbread as the police began to round up the gang.

The Devil and his theories apart, I often wonder how someone could motivate people to hold up a train, rob it and steal millions of pounds. Someone like me, a petty thief, would have some difficulty convincing people that I had an idea of robbing a train: most people would just have thought that I been putting too many illegal substances up my nose and would have dismissed me in the belief that I was suffering the side effects of an hallucinogenic drug.

• • •

I got to know Bruce after I interviewed him for a book I wrote with Angela Devlin called *Going Straight After Crime and Punishment*. This was a collection of stories about ex-offenders who had turned their lives around. We became friends and have remained so ever since. When I told Frank Longford about this he said, 'Why not invite Bruce to the House of Lords for afternoon tea?'!

As we sat in the magnificent tearooms, Bruce held Frank spellbound with tales of the robbery and other anecdotes. In all the years I knew Frank that was the only occasion I ever saw him lost for words. I remember Bruce telling Frank that he was introduced to Bobby Moore, captain of the English soccer team that won the World Cup in 1966. Apparently Moore said to Bruce, 'It's good to meet you, have you robbed any trains lately?' Quick as a flash Bruce replied, 'No, have you stolen any jewellery?', a reference to the time when the England squad were in Bogota in 1970, and Moore was arrested and accused of stealing a bracelet from the hotel shop - an allegation later wholly discredited. I asked Bruce what Moore's reaction had been. He said he had 'the right hump' and walked off muttering four letter words!

Bruce and I occupied different extremes of the prisoner hierarchy. On the inside he was tantamount to royalty: whilst I was the equivalent of a janitor or teaboy. In our own ways we were both failures: neither of us could avoid getting caught or stay out of prison for very long. I was reminded of the tale of the two villains who broke into a pub, helped themselves to a drink and a smoke and a game of darts. Pity was that they left their names on the scoreboard. Bruce and I were like that. We always seemed to leave our calling cards.

Now, many years on we had found common cause in our support for other ex-offenders and hence the interview for *Going Straight* I have already mentioned. Bruce told me that his 'conversion' began after he woke up one morning and realised that he could well spend the rest of his life behind bars. It was a shock to the system. He was getting too old for that. It is something that dawns on very many offenders at some stage in their lives and I have often wondered if there is a way of bringing this realisation about sooner rather than later. Bottling it for distribution so to speak!

I introduced Paul to Bruce and ordered a round of drinks whilst we waited for Bryan Gibson, my publisher, to arrive. Bryan, who was a lawyer until he became a publisher, has also been a good friend over the years. I remember first arriving at his Country House in north Hampshire in the 1990s and making my way along the sweeping gravel drive between the rhododendrons and yew hedges thinking, 'Just the kind of place I would have liked to burgle in my time'. But I contented myself with a 'review' of the security arrangements - a visual survey of the alarm system and pondering what enhancements might be sensible!

I remember that I had sent my manuscript on ahead. It had been spellchecked on my computer, but was still noticeably the work of someone who was dyslexic. Bryan decided to take a chance on it and the result was my first book, *I'm Still Standing*, which proved to be a giant step in firming up my self-esteem and establishing my new life on the right side of the law. I remember him putting down the telephone at the exact same moment that I entered his office: 'It was Lord Longford to ask whether you'd arrived safely . . . and to promise a Foreword'. That was Frank all over. Impeccable timing. As I mentioned in *Chapter 3*, it was the kind of unsung support that he gave so freely and unstintingly to so many people whom he thought could be redeemed, but which never hit the headlines.

• • •

Now that we were all gathered, a waiter led us upstairs to the dining-room - and yet more celebrities. The idea was to discuss over lunch a TV film that Paul wanted to make to coincide with the fortieth anniversary of the robbery, whilst Bryan was considering a book along the same lines if he could see a suitable angle. None of us was intending to reinvent the wheel but - let's us face it - none of the original gang was getting any younger and there were becoming fewer and fewer survivors! By the same token they might now be prepared to say or confirm things publicly that they would not have done in their younger days. There are a number of mysteries associated with the robbery, like who assaulted the driver Jack Mills, what happened to the money and whether there was a 'Mr Big' - who, if so, could well be still alive and quaking in his shoes.

• • •

'When you've lived in as many hotels as I have you'd give anything for a decent plate of bangers and mash . . . The one thing I craved when I was on-the-run was bangers and mash,' grumbled Bruce as he thumbed down the five star menu.

He described his life as a mix between that of James Bond and Monty Python: 'The robbery was such a challenge . . . but we were so stupid'. Like buying an open-top Austin Healey 3000 with wire wheels and paying in cash a few days after the robbery. There were other snippets. When the police threw a thirty mile cordon around Bridego Bridge, the scene of the robbery, he walked through it dressed as an angler, tipping his hat to them. He was picked up by an old couple in a Ford Anglia who insisted on berating him with exhortations such as 'Can you believe it, young man, a mail train has been robbed!', for which he slipped momentarily into Eric Idle in a headscarf mode: 'It was just up the road . . . Can you just believe it?'!

The thirty mile cordon was what caused the gang to quit their temporary hideout, Leatherslade Farm, early, leaving clues which the clean up team they had employed failed to deal with. There had always been a debate whether to head back to London straightaway after the robbery in a fleet of Jaguars as suggested by racing driver Roy James. Bruce ruled that they should not do so, but would return to the farm and hole up there until the heat subsided and to count the money. But the farm was just two miles inside the cordon and hence the gang's change of plan. Bruce did say that if they had adopted James's plan there might have been a different outcome. James himself was back on the track, racing in competition within days.

Boredom rather than being recognised was Bruce's downfall. 'I got fed up with wearing dark-glasses, only to discover that no-one knew who I was anyway!' On-the-run in New York he felt that he was a nonentity who could safely queue for bagels: he hardly needed to sneak around at all. In Mexico – as an ex-patriot and 'local' businessman - he was invited by the British Consulate to meet HRH the Prince of Wales, but politely declined. In South America - with his companions Buster Edwards and Charlie Wilson - he had, for cover, obtained a franchise to sell cigarette lighters and set about entertaining potential clients. 'We never sold many lighters, but we were big on receptions . . . We held one every other night just to keep ourselves occupied and so as to look busy'!

• • •

There has always been speculation about whether there was someone behind the scenes who was never brought to justice - in other words a 'Mr Big'. In his own book, *The Autobiography of a Thief* (Bantam Press, 1995), Bruce Reynolds describes how Gordon Goody knew a bent solicitor, Brian Field, who had defended both Gordon and Buster Edwards in the past. He went on to claim that Field not only defended criminals but also mixed with them. Field, so the story goes, introduced Goody and Edwards to a man known as 'The Ulsterman'. The meeting took place on a bench in Finsbury Park in north London. The Ulsterman told them about a train that travelled regularly between Glasgow and London carrying a large consignment of mailbags that could contain millions of pounds in used notes.

'Are you interested?' he asked, 'Can you do it?' Edwards and Goody were stunned at the scale of the job but told The Ulsterman that they could put a team together that could handle something of that size. The Ulsterman then gave them a detailed breakdown of the security arrangements and the timetable of events. Between fifty and eighty mailbags were transported in the high value package coach on the overnight train to London. These contained English banknotes spent in Scotland and which were being returned to the Bank of England. At holiday times there could be five times the usual number of sacks. Allegedly, it was The Ulsterman who told the gang that the train would be leaving Glasgow on the night of the robbery loaded with money.

'No-one has really confirmed whether or not there was a Mr Big?'

I put this to Bruce across the lunch table. It would be something of an exclusive if he were prepared to name Mr Big in the film or book. Bruce affected to look hurt – after all he was 'The Brains' behind the robbery, was he not, the only 'Mr Big'? I had, in fact, been given a name for The Ulsterman by an old underworld contact. 'Of course you know who The

Ulsterman is, don't you?' my informant had said - as if everyone else on the planet had already heard the news. Steeling my nerve, I spat out the name and asked Bruce whether this man - an outwardly respectable businessman and well-connected in certain spheres of British life - had bankrolled the robbery and pulled the strings. 'Yes, I've heard that name before,' said Bruce, '. . . never did work out where it came from' - with the casual air of someone who has probably had names rolled at him many times.[1]

The times they were a-changing and the early 1960s was a time of huge social and political upheaval and the breaking down of barriers. There was the appearance of the Beatles, the politico-sexual Profumo scandal, and tensions and demonstrations over censorship and sexual freedom. The Great Train Robbery seemed to add insult to injury as far as the loosening of the old values was concerned: heads were going to roll. Even the trial judge, Mr Justice Edmund Davies, was accused of being in the hands of the Establishment. John Daly was the only one to be acquitted.

'So what did you think to the thirty year sentences?,' I asked Bruce.
'Shook everyone rigid,' was his instant response.
'Regrets?'
'None.'
'Would you do it again if you had your time over?'
'It's like the Millennium Diamond . . . the Crown Jewels . . . '.

I took this to be misplaced nostalgia. Bruce and his south London Gang had pulled off several 'stunts' as he liked to call them. In one of these they had dressed in business suits and bowler hats and even carried umbrellas. Then they entered the vault as if they were the auditors - but made off with the loot. 'The Heathrow Airport Job', they called it. Bruce remembered to add that he had done his time for it.

'The problem with the Monty Python analogy is that during the train robbery someone actually got hurt?' I reminded him.

Initially there had been one real sticking point to the gang's plan. Who would drive the train from Sears Crossing where they planned to stop it, by fixing the railway signals, to Bridego Bridge where they would unload the loot? There is more to driving a train than meets the

---

[1] I discussed with the publishers the possibility of naming The Ulsterman in this book but was told that despite the Human Rights Act there are still certain risks associated with freedom of speech!

eye! Sheer coincidence located a driver. Bruce was visiting his friend, Ronnie Biggs. The pair had served time together and Ronnie was now living in Reigate, Surrey where he was employed as a carpenter (a trade which he had learned whilst serving his last prison sentence). Bruce told Ronnie that he was working on 'a big one' and happened to mention that he needed a train driver. At the time, Ronnie was working on a retired train driver's house - so he agreed to try and recruit him. Bruce said that he would guaranteed Ronnie at least £40,000 for his trouble. A week later, Bruce had the news that the driver was interested. Ronnie himself had one more stipulation: he wanted a piece of the action. Quite apart from what I have said about The Ulsterman, Ronnie Biggs wrote in his book, *Odd Man Out* (Bloomsbury, 1994) that three of the gang plus the train driver he recruited were never caught.

When the gang stopped the train at Sears Crossing, Roy James and another member started uncoupling the coaches while further members of the gang bundled David Whitby, the train's fireman, out of the cab. The driver, Jack Mills, attempted to put up some resistance so he was hit over the head, taken off the train and placed on the railway embankment where Charlie Wilson was waiting for him.

Ronnie Biggs claimed that Mills was on his feet looking groggy and bleeding from the head which Charlie Wilson was mopping with a white handkerchief. Charlie then said to him, 'You're okay, Dad, you're not badly hurt.' They sat on the grass verge beside the tracks and Charlie offered him a cigarette.

'I think you're a real gentleman,' Jack Mills said, according to Biggs.

'Do you want any money?, Charlie asked, 'We'll leave it on the grass verge'. Mills shook his head.

I once asked Bruce whether Jack Mills received any of the money but he did not confirm or deny it, he just smiled and rolled his eyes as if in disbelief. It seems to be a perverted way of thinking that he could be compensated with a share of stolen money.

Unbeknown to the gang the brake pressure of the train had fallen and temporarily demobilised the locomotive. To everyone's horror the stand-in driver had to wait for the pressure to rise again before he could move it forward. Panic started to sweep through the cab. Gordon Goody believed that the driver they had recruited was unable to drive the train, which was not true. It was simply that there was not enough brake pressure. Goody insisted they got Mills back into the cab. By then the pressure had risen so that when Mills was told to move the train to Bridego Bridge he was able to do so.

It has been argued by some people that the powers that be deliberately set out to discredit the gang as mindless thugs, so that they played up Jack Mills' injuries. He was photographed going into court in a wheelchair and pictures of him with his head in bandages appeared on the front pages of the newspapers. After he recovered, he was eventually placed on light duties with full pay. The press releases of the time state that because of the injuries he had sustained during the robbery he would never be able to return to full duties. He became the key figure in manipulating the 'monstrous' nature of the robbery. Peta Fordham, in her book, *The Robber's Tale*, tells how he had admitted to her that he was warned his pension was at stake if he showed any sympathy for the gang or indicated that they treated him well. He died in 1970 of leukaemia. A Home Office pathologist, following a post mortem, described this as natural causes. There are still people who say that his death was a direct result of or was hastened by the injuries he received. Talking to some railway workers - some of whom were not even born in 1963 - they showed much hatred towards Bruce and the gang. They thought that Jack Mills had actually been murdered during the course of the robbery.

In 1988, the film *Buster* was made, starring Phil Collins and Julie Walters. It was due to have a royal premiere with the Prince of Wales and Princess Diana in attendance. The proceeds were expected to exceed £100,000 which were to be donated to the Prince's Trust and Turning Point, two charities of which the Royal couple were patrons. However, Alexander Walker of the *Evening Standard* sent an open letter to the Prince stating that the film made a hero out of a criminal and alleged corruption by Her Majesty's Government. The royal couple withdrew from the premiere, even though this was twenty-five years after the robbery.

At lunch in the Grouch Club, Bruce goes into denial-mode. 'Driver Mills died seven years after the robbery, from unrelated causes – and in any event violence was never on the agenda. Someone panicked. Wouldn't you on a night like that?' But it remains unclear who did panic. Bruce himself has a reputation for being non-violent - which befits his studious, academic image. He has often been styled 'intellectual' and you only have to engage in conversation with him for a short time to realise that he is well read. He told us that that in prison he read anything and everything he could lay his hands on. He informed us that guns were at all times banned in the South London Gang, especially on the night of the robbery.

• • •

The three of us were then treated to an explanation of the pseudo-economics of crime, a criminal version of market forces. In a nutshell this amounts to 'Everyone wants their cut' and the fact that the price rises in proportion to the level of the hue and cry. So many people wanted a cut - or a bigger cut - as the proceeds of the train robbery passed from hand to hand that in the end they were worth only a tenth of their real value. 'A lot of money went missing . . . and who is going to tell the police?' 'Large chunks went missing after being found', Bruce added, explaining that by this he meant 'before they reached the police station!' In one instance this included a 'drop' at a telephone kiosk where, so Bruce claimed, the surveillance team made off with the holdall and its contents.

'Yes, I've been back to Bridego Bridge, Sears Common – and to Leatherslade Farm'.
'How could anyone plan such an audacious crime and leave amateurs to clean up?'
'That's the Monty Python bit, again'.
'So what do you do with two-and-a-half million pounds'.

Bruce said that at first the gang's reaction was one of disbelief. No one had seen that much money before. It took a day to count it all. There were piles of bank notes on tables, chairs and on the floor. As they were counting, some of them sang Tony Bennett's 'It's the Good Life'. Then followed a rendition of Gerry and the Pacemaker's 'I Like It'. They settled down to beans on toast - for those who were not too excited to eat. Some of the gang played Monopoly with real money. The Get-Out-of-Jail card cost a thousand pounds.

• • •

We also learned that the robbery had been planned for the day before. Posing as 'weekend soldiers' on a military training exercise and after everyone was in position and waiting for the train, the gang received a message that it was the wrong night. Bruce slips into Eric Idle-mode from 'Monty Python' again: 'I'm sorry, Mr Reynolds, it's not today, it's tomorrow!' This caused a 24-hour delay and put everyone on tenterhooks. Then, as if an earlier question was still troubling his thoughts, he added that the resulting jumpiness was another possible explanation as to why driver Mills got hurt.

Bruce was eventually arrested after five years on-the-run. Privately, he told me that he first returned to England to rob another train but the plan had gone awry! Appropriately enough for someone who likes to describe his criminal career as part Monty Python, his downfall came not in some distant, exotic location but in Torquay where he was living a mundane and anonymous existence. He was sentenced to twenty-five years in prison of which he served twelve, mainly at Wandsworth Prison, where he had more or less iconic status amongst the prisoners. He was released in 1978. The gang as a whole received sentences ranging from three to thirty years, in total over three hundred years. Many saw this as undue retribution, vengeful and little to do with just desserts. The sentences became one trigger for wide-ranging changes to the parole system.

• • •

For some people there is a dubious attraction about 'big time crime'. I learned from another underworld contact that a friend of Bruce's and an acquaintance of mine, Joey Pyle, hid Bruce in his flat in Clapham for several months after the robbery. In the late-1950s and early-1960s my brother, Fred, was a bookie's runner. In those days, it was illegal to place a bet anywhere other than on the racecourse. Bookmakers would employ people to collect and pay out bets illegally. Fred would stand on the street corner outside my school and collect bets and take them to the bookie. In the evening he would return to pay out the winnings. Every now and again the police would have a purge in an attempt to clear up the illegal gambling, often making token arrests. This never stopped it, very much as it is with drug dealing today. Once the police close down one source, another springs up.

Like the drug dealers of today, Fred saw himself as providing a service. Many of the drug dealers I have worked with as a probation officer do not believe that they are committing a real criminal offence. They tell me that that they do not steal from or rob people. People come to them. The dealers ask, 'What harm am I doing'? It is well documented that a huge amount of crime is fuelled by addiction, whether to drugs, alcohol or gambling. There will always be people willing to cash in on any demand and to rationalise their activities as Joey and Fred did.

Fred would frequent the drinking dens of the local criminal fraternity. One such place was Max's drinking club in Tooting, where he took me for the first time in January 1960. Seated at a table in the corner were Joey Pyle, Peter 'Ginger' Tilley and a couple of other shady characters. These people were notorious gangsters who were into organized crime in a big way. They had an air of mystery about them and it was clear they had respect from other customers in the club.

Joey was a friend of the Kray twins, but somehow also managed to maintain a relationship with the Kray's arch rivals, the Richardson brothers. By the end of the 1960s both these feuding gangs were in prison, leaving Joey controlling most of the rackets in London. Over the next thirty years he was arrested more than fifty times on charges ranging from robbery and firearms offences to murder and drug smuggling - but each time he was prosecuted I would see him walk out of court scot-free.

These were defining moments for me: the buzz, the mystique, the lure of easy money and 'getting away with it'. People like Joey became role models. My path was set. But somehow I never completely made it into their world, only to its fringes from where I looked on in awe. I would drink with Joey's brother, Teddy, and got involved in some criminal enterprises with his cousin, Terry White. We would congregate in the St Helier Arms, once dubbed by the media 'the most violent public house in London'. It was the scene of drive-by shootings and gang fights.

One evening I was drinking in the saloon bar with a few friends including Jack 'The Hat' McVitie who I mentioned in *Chapter 1* and who was murdered by the Kray twins. Trouble was always destined to follow The Hat around like a lost dog. I got caught up in this once when he was drinking with our circle. Someone walked into the public bar of the St Helier Arms and fired a sawn-off shot-gun, missing The Hat by inches but nicking a couple of other villains in the legs. But we were hardened to such things - or so we liked to pretend to ourselves. We carried on drinking until the police arrived, explained that we were all in the toilet or nipping down to the betting shop at the time. When they cordoned off the bar we simply moved on to the pub down the road. The police eventually had the St Helier Arms closed down. It was later demolished and houses built on the site.

• • •

After several months of enjoying Joey Pyle's hospitality, Bruce Reynolds and his family slipped out of the UK and eventually ended up in Mexico. Bruce told me that he could have gone to South Africa where the language would not have been such a problem but he chose Mexico because, as he put it, 'It had more of a romantic ring to it'. He was later joined there by Buster Edwards and his family. I find it amazing that although the train robbers were wanted by police around the world, not only were they able to travel unnoticed but they also took their families with them. I doubt that this could happen nowadays, what with Interpol, Europol and other forms of international partnership. Major crime is increasingly of the electronic variety - or 'cybercrime - so that the modern-day villain can sit at home anonymously behind a computer and beaver away at emptying people's bank accounts around the globe. The Tommy Butlers and Jack Slippers of today - the detectives who pursued the robbers - are probably all computer nerds.

June, Buster Edwards's wife, had had enough of living in Mexico so she returned to England with their young daughter, leaving Buster there. In 1966, he too returned to London and gave himself up, hoping to do a deal with the authorities. Unable to do so, he was duly sentenced to fifteen years. He was released in 1975 and for the next nineteen years had a flower stall outside London's Waterloo station where he became a tourist attraction. One cold Tuesday morning in 1994, he was found dead in a lock-up garage by his brother. He had hanged himself after going on a drinking binge. There was no obvious explanation for his suicide other than money problems.

I asked Bruce what he thought. He said that Buster had been unhappy for some time and had hated going straight. It does not suit everyone. He had been a criminal for the sheer hell of it. He got a big kick out his lifestyle. The events can be compared to a footballer who has reached the end of his career, when there is a big void in life. Buster missed the buzz and the camaraderie, however thin the veneer.

• • •

After serving four months of his thirty year sentence, Charlie Wilson escaped from Winson Green Prison, Birmingham. Three people broke into the prison, unlocked his cell and took him out wearing just his vest. They hid him in a specially adapted oil tanker and drove off. Within hours, he was out of the country on his way to Canada. He set up home with his family just outside Montreal, where he would remain for the next three and a half years. His whereabouts were only discovered when his wife Pat telephoned her family back in England

It was not long before chief superintendent, Tommy Butler, who had been leading the hunt for the robbers, turned up on Charlie's doorstep in the company of a large troop of Canadian Mounted Police and brought him back to the UK to finish his sentence. I worked with Charlie in the laundry at Coldingley Prison where I found him to be a warm individual with that wicked brand of humour that is brought out in some people by the sheer futility of prison life. Charlie was the last of the train robbers to be released on parole from Pentonville Prison, in November 1978. There was a picture of him on the front page of most of the tabloids with a sack of sugar on his shoulder coming out of the kitchens.

Six years later Charlie Wilson moved to Spain where he had a villa in Marbella. One day in 1990, a man called. He had a London accent and wore a grey tracksuit and a baseball cap. It was clear that Charlie knew him well because he let him in and they went to the pool area to talk. Pat, Charlie's wife, was in the house when she heard raised voices, and then two loud bangs which turned out to be gunfire. She ran into the garden but the visitor had gone. Charlie was staggering towards the pool. He had been shot twice, once in the neck, severing his carotid artery and a second bullet went into his mouth and out through the back of his head. He died shortly afterwards. There was wild speculation that the shooting was 'an execution' carried out by a rival drugs gang.

Bruce is convinced that Charlie was not involved in drugs. They had practically grown up together so he knew Charlie very well. He believes he would not have got involved in that kind of thing. 'He moved to Spain for a quiet life away from the aggro of the South London villainy,' said Bruce. The truth is that no-one really knows why he was killed but every now and again some fresh theory raises its head about who he had crossed to such an extent that they wanted him dead.

• • •

Madam Tussaud's created waxwork models of both Charlie Wilson and Ronald Biggs, who escaped from Wandsworth Prison eleven months later. Ronnie explored various options. He favoured the idea of being airlifted out by helicopter, thinking that this had a romantic feel - and it would rub salt into the already festering wound in the official backside. But he took advice from another inmate, Dennis Stafford, who had attracted notoriety when he escaped from Dartmoor in the 1950s. He told Ronnie that when he was in Chelmsford Prison he was in the exercise yard when a helicopter flew low over the prison. Immediately, two prison officers got hold of him and he was back inside before he knew what was happening. Much to Ronnie's disappointment the helicopter plot had to be abandoned.

However, the prison grapevine swung into action with messages being passed to and fro between the prison and the outside world and a plan was hatched for Ronnie to go over the wall from the exercise yard. At five past three one afternoon, Ronnie was in the yard of D-wing when a furniture van pulled alongside the wall. An accomplice appeared on top of the wall wearing a nylon stocking over his head and lowered a rope ladder down to Ronnie. Three others scaled the wall while prisoners in the exercise yard fought with prison staff to allow them time to make their escape.

That escape began a thirty-five-year long hue and cry with Ronnie being chased around the world for the first five of those years. From England, Ronnie went to France, where he had plastic surgery and then he and his family set off for Australia. He had to flee Australia, leaving them there, and ended up in Brazil where he was to spend the next thirty years. In that time, there were attempts by Scotland Yard to extradite him. There were also kidnap attempts by bounty hunters but all failed. He met a Brazilian beauty by the name of Raimunda Fernand and three years later she gave birth to their son, Michael. With these family responsibilites in Brazil Biggs could no longer be sent home.

Raimunda now runs an export business in Switzerland. She walked out on Ronnie, leaving him with their son whom he raised from the age of eleven months. She never forgave him for lying about his identity or for the occasion when Brazilian police broke into their home with machine guns, looking for the proceeds of the robbery. Many years later, Michael said of him,

> He was my father, mother, friend and teacher; everything I know I learned from my Dad. We were, and are, very, very close, he instilled in me a sense of right and wrong, he always told me never, ever to break the law.

Bruce and other members of the gang have always insisted that Ronnie's role in the robbery was peripheral. He joined in at the last minute and the first time he touched any of the loot was at Leatherslade Farm.

Over the years, Ronnie became an international celebrity. He signed record deals with the punk band, the Sex Pistols, made a film about his life and wrote a couple of his books. British tourists would ask him to pose for pictures and sign autographs. He seemed to be giving the authorities the old two finger salute.

Bruce gave me Ronnie's telephone number and told me that if I mentioned his name to Ronnie he felt sure he would give me an interview for *Going Straight*. After all, his was an unusual case: a major criminal leading as normal a life as possible in the full glare of the world's press, but essentially an ex-offender even though his sentence was still outstanding. Quite a specimen!

I phoned Ronnie and as soon as I mentioned Bruce we got on like a house on fire and he was happy to talk to me. To begin with this involved several telephone conversations with him. We swopped stories about Wanno and joked about the food. After a while, it came clear to me that there was far more to him than the 'loveable rogue' of popular myth. Beneath the outward bravado lay melancholy and introspection. He was seventy years old. All his co-defendants were now free men and it was twenty years since Charlie Wilson, the last to be released, had headed off for a new life. There was a strong sense of loneliness and isolation. He lived like a king but was still in exile. I felt I was on to something.

I happened to mention these conversations to a TV producer whom I trusted enough not to sensationalise the whole thing. His ears immediately pricked up. He said his people had been trying to get an interview with Ronnie for years. He said that if I could get it for them they would be willing to fly me and a film crew to Rio de Janiero. I spoke to Ronnie and he agreed. He said any friend of Bruce's was a friend of his, and generously said he would put us all up in his home. The one condition was that he and I were to be filmed walking down the famous Copa Cabana beach.

Ten days before the visit, I phoned Ronnie to check the details. The phone was answered by his son, Michael who told me that his father had suffered a stroke. He was seriously ill and unable to speak. I asked Michael to send my best wishes to his father and asked if I could do anything in the UK for them. The film company took just minutes to decide to end the project and I could not really include Ronnie in the book without the planned one-to-one interview. Later, after suffering two further two strokes, Ronnie induced Bruce to broker a deal with the *Sun* newspaper to fly him back to England to give himself up.

I gave various radio interviews at the time saying that I did not believe the prevailing view that he was seeking to sponge off the

National Health Service. I think that, just like some of the other robbers, he becoming more and more aware that his time was limited. The strokes had simply brought this to a head.

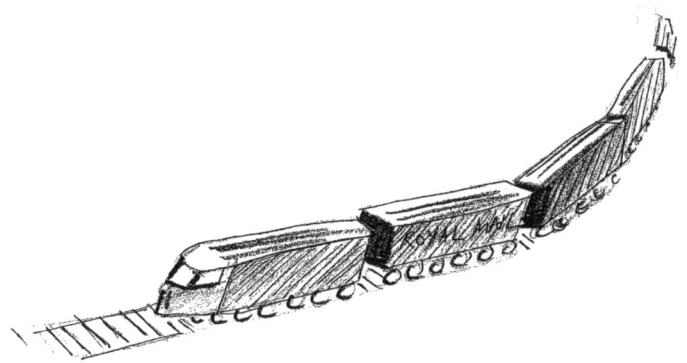

Ronnie is now back in prison and even frailer after heart attacks and further strokes. He is too weak to walk and in a wheelchair. No longer able to talk, he uses an alphabet board for communicating. He is fed by a tube into his stomach. For more than three years he was held in Belmarsh Prison, a top security establishment in South London. Michael said that some of the other inmates had been helping him out including by doing his ironing for him but the governor put a stop to that. The authorities were becoming worried that he would become a cult figure, and had decreed 'limited contact', in effect a form of solitary confinement. Even Jeffrey Archer, writing in his *Prison Diary*, felt sorry for him. It is difficult to know what the public really thinks, but the conundrum presented by the plight of this now fragile human being - who has until now evaded justice for a major crime - has no easy answers. But in many ways the public has already had its revenge.

• • •

The Groucho Club was almost empty by now and we were the only four left in the restaurant. The 'luvvies' had all gone back to their rehearsals, or wherever luvvies go in the afternoon. As we leaned in low across the table and kept our voices down to prevent our conversation echoing around the room we must have looked like four conspirators waiting for the Devil to appear and make us an offer. Bruce beat him to it: 'It's the intellectual challenge, you see. Doing something that no-one else has . . . Yes, I wouldn't exactly rule it out if the right challenge came along. Any ideas?'

CHAPTER 8

Restorative Justice

Wanted!

CHAPTER 8

Restorative Justice

I had arrived early and was standing outside Wandsworth Prison in London - 'Wanno' for short - waiting to enter. I was there as a probation officer to interview an inmate for a pre-sentence report following his recent trial and conviction for a string of offences. As I turned towards the main gate, a prisoner was being released into the warm August sunshine. There is a narrow door in one corner of the gate and he was stepping sideways through it - out of the darkness and into the light so to speak. He was hesitant, looking around a lot, scanning up and down the road. His faced showed the same anxiety that mine did when I was let out of that same door for the last time twenty-five years earlier. He shielded his eyes against the sun like a rabbit caught in the headlights of an approaching car - with no idea what to expect or which way to dart. Just as I had done, he was leaving the safety and security of an institution for a world of uncertainty.

'Good morning!' I chirped reassuringly.

The man answered with a contemptuous stare. The look I used to give strangers. He was still on his guard, suspicious of everybody and everything. In prison even a well-intended 'Hello' or sideways glance can be taken as a threat, accusation or mistrust. I knew exactly where he was coming from.

For a split second, as we passed each other by, the past and the present merged. It was uncanny. This pitiable, dishevelled guy *was* me. He had no one to meet him. Perhaps he had nowhere to go. Nobody to care. His haunted expression marked him out as someone destined for the revolving doors of imprisonment, release, imprisonment, release. I watched him disappear like a ghost of my former self down the Heathfield Road and wondered which direction he would choose at the T-junction. He paused, looked both ways, then rather than heading towards the outskirts of the town turned right towards the shops, pubs and the lure of temptation. How long would *he* survive on the outside?

• • •

I had been released from that very same gate numerous times with nowhere to go. I was let out one day with a discharge grant of just a few pounds in my pocket and a travel warrant that would just about get me across London. I had no actual home or address but hoped that someone would offer a bed for the night. I need not have concerned myself. I never made it that far. I too stopped off at the nearest pub and by midnight I was in a drunken stupor, broke and back in a cell. I had been arrested for trying to steal a car to use in a burglary. I was kept in the police station overnight and the following morning was up before the stipendiary magistrate.[1] I copped a quick plea of 'guilty', was given another six months and by the evening I had been transported in the meat wagon back to the familiar and comfortable surroundings of Wanno. I would not need to worry about a roof over my head for the next few months. The food was just about bearable and I would be able to puff on the odd roll-up.

The prison has two parts, both Victorian in the radial style. The main prison has four large wings: A, B, C and D. The smaller part of the prison has three wings: E, F and G. When it opened in 1851 female prisoners were held in the smaller of the wings. I spent most of my time there on E-wing. By that time in my life I was destined to become a hopeless 'old lag'. I was well over the shock of imprisonment that hits the young and the first timers.

• • •

After casting my mind back to those early days I returned to the present and remembered that just a few days earlier in 2004 the terrible news broke that Adam Rickwood had became the youngest person to die in custody in the UK at the age of fourteen. He had committed suicide by hanging himself with the laces from a pair of trainers his mother had taken in for him thirty-six hours earlier during the previous day's visit. This was the last time she saw him alive. Adam was in custody waiting to go to court on a comparatively minor offence of wounding. What would have driven a young, small boy (he was only five foot two inches tall) and too young even to shave to commit suicide?

I will never forget the gut-wrenching feeling I had when, in my new life, I arrived at the office one Monday morning, only to find that one of the young people I had been working with had committed suicide in his cell over the weekend. I had overwhelmingly mixed emotions of sadness and anger. Sadness, because I had come to know him - worked with him and his family, visited his home and been a part of his and his family's lives - and anger at the waste of human life and the existence of a system that lets vulnerable people down. These reactions combined with a crushing sense of inadequacy and guilt. 'I should have done more to prevent it,' was my foremost thought, followed by memories of the last time I had visited him.

I blamed myself for not picking up 'the signals' that something untoward was about to happen. I felt like resigning on the spot. But you

---

[1] As district judges used to be called.

cannot do that. You have to soldier on: continue to work with those feelings whilst contacting the relatives. Then you have to close the file and send it off for minute inspection. If it does not stand up to the scrutiny there might be disciplinary action. But I can understand what drove Adam because I have been there myself. Prison itself can seem like the end of the world anyway.

There will always be tragedies like Adam's and the doomed prisoner I came face-to-face with that August morning - unless, that is, we can somehow change our mindset about how we deal with those people in our midst who break the law. The existing system offers a poor deal both to vulnerable first-timers and hardened offenders. As Oscar Wilde said, prisons are built 'with bricks of shame'.

• • •

I wrote in *Chapter 3* about how the Longford Trust came to be set up. The third annual Longford Lecture was to be given by Archbishop Desmond Tutu. When we learned that he had agreed to come to England and to give the lecture there was enormous excitement. It would be styled 'Truth, Restoration and Reconciliation'. When the time came, the venue, Church House in Westminster - where the main hall is circular with seating in tiers all around - was packed to the rafters with the great and the good!

The archbishop created a real sense of occasion. He is small in stature but his energy inexhaustible. His sharp eyes are almost hypnotic and he is a mesmerising speaker. It was hard to believe that he was then 71 years old, judging from the energy and enthusiasm with which he addressed his audience and answered questions from the floor. I spoke with his personal assistant who is some thirty years the archbishop's junior, who told me Desmond Tutu leads such a vigorous lifestyle that he struggles to keep up with him!

It is around ten years since Archbishop Tutu became the first chair of the Truth and Reconciliation Commission in South Africa that has since transformed the lives of millions. Simply to be in his presence was an honour - and as I helped behind the scenes on the day I could hardly believe that an ex-con like me was rubbing shoulders with this great man! But I am sure he would not have seen it that way any more than Frank Longford would have done. As the evening progressed I could see Frank in my mind's eye rising from his seat to ask some incisive question or other and then to argue the toss - and at the reception afterwards, mingling with and haranguing the guests.

The Archbishop told us, 'The South African judicial system operates to free people who commit crimes if they make a full disclosure but there are those who ask, "What about justice?"' It is clear that most people who ask that question think in terms of only one kind of justice, retributive justice - which is what the guilty receive overwhelmingly the world over. The purpose of retributive justice is to ensure that the offender is *punished*. Its advocates point to the biblical injunction of 'an eye for an eye' as justification.

If we build our criminal justice systems solely on notions of retribution we end up with what we have now in the UK - a crisis in our penal system, with record numbers of people incarcerated. Similarly, the penal systems of most countries have failed to stem crime and recidivism.

I have already mentioned in *Chapter 4* how even when matters are taken to extremes in countries that still have the death penalty there is still no evidence to suggest a drop in crimes, including crimes of violence and murder. It is the same with punitive laws. Since the Labour Government came to power in 1997, it has passed around 700 new laws in its attempts to be 'tough on crime and tough on the causes of crime.' You only have to ask people who are living on run down council estates around the UK if there has been a reduction in the crime or in anti-social behaviour: they will tell you that their lives are still blighted. It is only when a community gets together and starts to make some kind of connection with those who are committing crimes that any kind of success seems to be achieved: when both parties see each other as people.

David Davis MP, the shadow home secretary, told the Conservative Party Conference in Bournemouth in 2004 that there were just 100,000 persistent offenders committing half the offences in the country. He estimated that 15,000 of them were already in prison - and that therefore the Tories intended to build more prisons to accommodate the remaining 85,000! In his next breath, he went on to say that when the Tories come to power, they intend to make available more treatment centres for drug addicts who commit offences to fund their drug habits. I think that the majority of the 85,000 people he wants to 'bang up' are just such addicts. So do we need more prisons or more rehabilitation centres?

I have already described the revolving door of prison. My own experience - from my past life and now in my work with offenders - is that prison is a self-perpetuating industry that largely feeds on the kind of fodder that people like myself provided. Yes, there are people who need to be locked away for all our sakes, but with the vast majority of offenders it is other things that need to be tackled. This is confirmed by the official re-conviction rates. These show that almost eighty per cent of people sent to prison will re-offend within two years of their release. Clearly, people do not learn from their mistakes simply by being punished.

Albert Einstein once said, 'The significant problems we face cannot be solved by the same level of thinking that created them.' What he was implying is that there needs to be a shift in the way we think. Like the paradigm shift that was needed with regard to my own offending behaviour. What brought about that shift was the fact that I finally wanted enough to go straight - to move away from the security of my prison cell and to try to become a productive member of society. To go from being wanted by the police to being wanted for myself, if you like. But the most important thing is that *I* wanted it.

But what triggered it? I had committed hundreds of burglaries in my time, but only one 'creeper burglary' - meaning one where I entered a house when the occupants were tucked up in beds asleep. At the time I was so desperate for drugs that I would have done anything to get my next fix. But I was already so 'stoned' that I woke up my victims as I was getting into the house, and I fled empty-handed. I can still remember today their panic stricken voices shouting for help. It had a profound effect on me. Looking back, I can see that it was a defining moment. Those screams had somehow managed to pass right under my radar. They by-passed all my defences and were more powerful than any drug I was taking. They touched a nerve. I had a twinge of conscience, something that had not happened before.

Until then, I would insulate myself from my victims. When I broke into a house I would turn over any photographs of the occupiers because I did not want to have anything to with them. I was stealing inanimate objects and I would distance these from their owners who had no doubt worked hard for them. That way I avoided responsibility. When I was arrested and later in court it would be an automatic and mechanical process. All I had to do was confirm my name and address (if I had one at the time) and say whether I was 'guilty' or 'not guilty'. Often, I did not even have to do that. My lawyer would do it for me and then make a speech in mitigation on my behalf. I might nod my head or mumble something incoherent if pressed about the error of my ways by the judge or magistrate.

The victims of my crimes had no or little involvement in the court process. I pleaded guilty - which I would usually do to avoid a longer sentence as part of a tactical game in which the only thing that mattered was when I would be back on the streets again. My victims would not even get as far as the courtroom unless they came and sat in the public gallery, which was rare. Remorse never came into it.

This is how, in the UK, the victim's role is marginalised. 'Their' crime may even become 'lost' in a list of offences that the offender asks the court to take into consideration - or 'TICs' as they are known. It never even gets a mention. Again, for the offender, it is all part of the game: getting the least punitive sentence. There is no making of amends.

If the accused person pleads 'not guilty', the victim may get to court to give evidence at the trial. During this experience he or she can be victimised all over again by the cross-examination of some sharp lawyer. Victims of crime are often completely disillusioned with the way they are treated even though there are now special schemes to try and look after them and organizations like Victim Support and the Victims of Crime Trust. But when a crime is committed, it is deemed to be have been committed not against them but *against the state*. When I was sent to prison, I would feel really sorry *for myself*. I had no notion of the misery my behaviour caused to other people - not until I heard those screams.

• • •

Even with the severest punishment crime can leave unresolved issues that can lie dormant in the mind of a victim for years. During one of the radio phone-ins that I described in *Chapter 5* one caller told me he been burgled twenty years earlier and he and his family were still re-living the experience. Even after all this time they were still searching around car-boot sales and charity shops in the hope that they might one day find his late grandmother's wedding ring. The family had not been able to have 'closure'.

The existing system breeds conflict. Questions remain unanswered and the victim cannot move on. His or her sense of security is shattered, and victims have a tendency to blame themselves for what happened. They relive the crime in their minds over and over again and they can remain in that state for decades. Perhaps the reason why such people line up to appear in audience discussion programmes is so that they can at last vent their anger, 'get it off their chest'!

• • •

There is a way that the victim can play a more active and positive role. This is through an aspect of restorative justice. Restorative justice is a concept concerned with repairing the overall harm to individuals and the community rather than wreaking revenge and retribution. If it can work for an entire nation as it did in South Africa - in the sense of 'Truth and Reconciliation' - then how much more hope there must be at a more mundane and everyday level. It is not a new idea. It dates back to Anglo-Saxon times. Well before the Normans invaded England, it was a base for Roman Law - and was built into the earliest known written law, the Code of Hammurabi which dates back to 2000 BC. It has been practised in countries as far apart as Australia and Iceland and is often linked to less sophisticated communities such as the Maoris of New Zealand where the overall well-being of everyone - and resolving conflict - is a key priority for a tight-knit community.

In the UK there have been a number of restorative justice schemes that run alongside court proceedings and sentencing and that target young offenders. They bring together people involved in the offence and the offender's life to look at ways of repairing the harm he or she has done and preventing crime in the future.

Such schemes are gradually being extended to older offenders. Under some of them - and where the victim agrees to it - he or she is brought face-to-face with the perpetrator who has to explain to the victim why he or she committed the offence. The victim is then in a position to explain the impact that the offender's behaviour has had on him or her and his or her family. It is a very powerful process that I have found does tend to bring closure in its wake for both victim and offender. The offender is confronted with the aftermath of his or her behaviour, which in many instances has a profound impact on his or her attitude towards re-offending. It is a powerful experience.

There are sceptics. They believe that such meetings are a soft option or a further intrusion into the victim's private life, or that if the offender offers an apology then no more action is taken. Here they are misinformed, because restorative justice is not a stand-alone solution: it is incorporated into other sentences, particularly if the offender receives a custodial sentence. It can be a quite liberating experience for the victim to see the person who was responsible for turning their world upside down in prison and to express what damage that person has inflicted on them. It helps to start the essential healing process.

Under existing practice, such a meeting - sometimes called a restorative conference - can only be held if all parties agree. I am of the opinion that only the victim should have the choice whether or not to take part if a perpetrator is sentenced to a community sentence and the court feels it appropriate that the offender should be required to attend such a conference. There should, for example, be a condition in a community order that - subject to what the victim thinks - the offender and victim are to have a meeting. If the offender does not meet that requirement, he or she could face breach proceedings, and be re-sentenced.

Where an offender is in prison or a young offender institution, a conference can be set up 'on the inside' even if the victim is unwilling to take part. This works by having a victim of a similar offence sitting in, as if by proxy. A least the victim can have a report and will get some sort of closure - whilst the offender is confronted with the damage done by their *type* of behaviour. As I have said, my own views flow from direct personal experience of waking up to the existence of my victims. I think such procedures would have stopped me in my tracks sooner if they had existed then.

When he was prime minster, John Major suggested that as a society we needed to 'condemn more and understand less'. I have had many conversations with victims of crime. Many have a burning desire to understand why the offender acted in the way they did. If we adopt John Major's approach, we shut the door in the victim's face, whilst he or she is desperately searching to try and make head and tail, rhyme and reason of what happened. Of course we must condemn criminal behaviour and people who break the law should be sentenced by the courts, but victims should be brought more centre stage. They should not be 'forgotten people'.

• • •

Many years ago, I was working as a duty officer in a probation hostel. When I was on duty, I would sleep at the hostel and eat with the residents. One evening I was clearing away the supper dishes and chatting with one of the residents. The conversation turned to his offence.

'Bob, I am not going to commit any more burglaries.'
'You don't have say what you think I want to hear.'
'No, straight up, Bob, I mean it,' he replied.

Then he went on to tell me about his last offence. He had broken into a house and was gathering all the valuable property he could find when the owner returned. A fight ensued in which the burglar received a 'good hiding' from the householder before the police arrived to arrest him. It was not the beating he received that made him think twice about breaking into houses - because that is a risk you take if you get caught bang to rights in someone's home - but it was the fact that he was confronted by his victim. Like me, he began to understand that the inanimate objects he was stealing and which he would sell for a fraction of their true and 'hard earned' value were priceless family heirlooms. Being confronted by the victim was enough to make him take a long, hard look at what he was doing. As far as I know, he has not come to the attention of the courts again.

On another occasion I was interviewing a young man in Feltham Young Offender Institution. He was awaiting sentence for a number of burglaries. I had to interview him for a pre-sentence report. I went though the statements of the inhabitants of the house he had broken into. There were two young children in bed and we read what they said about the impact of his behaviour on them. One was awake and lay in her bed frozen with fear, believing that the burglar was going to kill her. As we continued the young man broke into tears. He said that he did not mean them any harm. He told me that he been smoking crack-cocaine and had little recollection of committing the offence.

We moved on to the mother's statement in which she explained that her husband worked away a great deal and that on the night in question she was at home alone apart from her two daughters. Since the time of the offence she had suffered a nervous breakdown and had been permanently on medication. Her husband had been forced to change his job which meant a drop in income. The home for which they had worked so hard had to be put on the market because she was so traumatised that she could no longer stay there on her own.

When we had finished going through the statement, the prisoner was distraught. For an inmate to show emotion in the visits room in the presence of other inmates is unheard of. But there was this young man sobbing uncontrollably. When he managed to compose himself, he asked me if there was anything he could do to try and 'put things right'. He was almost begging me to help him to make amends. He received, quite rightly, a substantial custodial sentence. In my report, I proposed that while he served his sentence he should also attend a restorative justice conference.

• • •

During a three-year secondment to my local youth offending team (or 'YOT' as we call it), I often wrote reports on young offenders. I would write about the impact that their offence had had on their victim. I have come to believe that when writing a pre-sentence report, the probation officer should, whenever possible, interview the victim and report on his or her feelings to the court thereby allowing the court to focus more on the damage that the crime has caused to the people involved. As it is, courts tend to focus mainly on punishment rather than repairing the damage that offences cause to victims of crime.

Einstein was master at putting things in a nutshell. The story goes that his doctorate was rejected by his university and he was asked to 'write rather more', so he took his thesis back and added just one incisive sentence. The award was then given. So I will add just one more sentence here on restorative justice. We should do this sooner rather than later!

CHAPTER 9

What on Earth will Happen Now?

CHAPTER 9

What on Earth will Happen Now?

There is nothing I enjoy more in my spare time nowadays than to put my Jack Russell, Bizzo, in the car - we call him Bizzo because he is 'the business' - and drive the short distance to the University of Reading campus where I can let him off the lead. In the grounds of the university there is an ornamental lake that is picturesque and habitat to all sorts of wildlife. Everyone needs peace and quiet now and again and when I am walking Bizzo I can leave the world behind for a time. Apart from when he is pestering me to throw a stick for him. I suppose that I more than the other dog owners I meet and touch my cap to am grateful that I have the freedom to do such simple things. You cannot take the dog for a walk when you are in prison! Neither can you do much else unless it complies with the Prison Rules.

• • •

Looking back over my life, I have come to realise what an astonishing journey it has been: my early years of misery and deprivation; the many years spent in prison; my time at university; and fifteen years as a probation officer - as well as the in-between-times when I have acted as a security consultant or media pundit. The speaking circuit has taken me across Europe and America and I have also gained great fulfilment from my writing and by taking part in training courses and community programmes of various kinds.

My media activities continue to bubble along. Picture this: it was 11.15 in the evening and I was in bed reading a book when my mobile telephone sprang to life. Getting a call at that time of night could only mean one thing, or so I thought - that one of the kids was stuck for a lift and needed picking up at the railway station! But when I thought about it they were all at home. So who could be calling at this ungodly hour? It turned out to be the BBC World Service wanting an interview there and then, on the spot. I told them to call me back on the landline.

They wanted to ask me about a theory that some scientists in the USA had come up with that people should leave food out for burglars. Not as some philanthropic or kind hearted gesture, or, worse, to poison them, but so that DNA could be obtained by forensic analysts from the leftovers! They had even suggested that the best foods for this were pizzas, apples and carrots. Well if people will come up with such groundbreaking ideas it is not for me to spike their pudding. I told the interviewer that I thought it was 'a blinding idea'! Not all, but some burglars do help themselves to food when they are in a house. I occasionally did, especially if I was coming off amphetamines. They are quite an appetite suppressant and the hunger backlash can be enormous. I was often ravenous. When I got into a house I would head straight for the fridge or fruit bowl. It has even been known for intruders to help themselves to a fry-up! There was no such thing as DNA technology during my time as a burglar. Had there been, there would have been ample evidence to see me put me away for a long time!

The World Service interview lasted for about five minutes. I never even got out of bed. When it was over I put the telephone back on the hook, switched off the light, turned over and fell sound asleep. A couple of days later a cheque landed on mat. Who needs to be a criminal?!

• • •

When I think about the achievements in my life the first and foremost must be managing to convince Sue to marry me. I often wonder how I pulled it off! When I first met her I had been out of prison a little over two years and had been sober only a few months. Not exactly an ideal catch, if you will pardon a statement of the obvious!

And yet there was this beautiful young woman, who came from a middle-class background and who had been privately educated, actually taking an interest in me. I am convinced that she must have had men queuing-up to date her and they must have been far more suitable for her - and would have offered far better prospects - than I. We have now shared a close, meaningful and loving relationship for over twenty years and have five wonderful kids and a great little grandson. Me a grandfather? It came as a shock to someone who was still wondering when adolescence was going to end. There was a time when I would have been incapable of rearing a goldfish. As my former cell mates might have said, 'You pulled off a right little coup there, Bobby boy'. They would be right.

Being invited to places like Downing Street, the House of Lords, Eton College and the Oxford Union helped to boost my ever hungry ego, but the greatest personal satisfaction has come from being invited to help out by giving a talk or presentation in a prison. I have visited many prisons doing this, but lately have been going into Reading Gaol, my local nick, which to give it its full and official title is 'Her Majesty's Prison and Young Offender Institution Reading'. It is of course world famous due to its most celebrated former occupant, the nineteenth century playwright, poet and socialite Oscar Wilde - who was imprisoned there for two years for 'the love that dare not speak its name', homosexuality. One of the prison officers at Reading is currently working on a book about the place, its history and the true background to Wilde's masterpiece *The Ballad of Reading Gaol* - which contains so many terms and expressions that we still use today in the criminal justice sphere.[1] I cannot wait to read it.

Wilde arrived at Reading Gaol in November 1894 and was there for two years under a brutal regime of hard labour. Had he been around today he would no doubt have emerged as a chat show host and been invited onto programmes such as 'Question Time' or 'Have I Got News for You?', the weekly BBC 2 TV news quiz. He may even have had his own series. As it was, he went to live in obscurity in France, his health broken by his experience of imprisonment, though not his mental faculties, something that the ballad, which was written after his release, clearly testifies to. There is a 'Wilde aura' about the place even now, because so much of what he had to say connects with what we do to prisoners today on a daily basis.

My role when I am at the prison is in connection with the ASDAN programme, which stands for Award Scheme Deployment and Accreditation Network. It is a personal development scheme for inmates which requires them to take part in offending behaviour programmes. Their age range is eighteen to twenty-one inclusive. It is a time in their lives when they are probably most vulnerable to influences that may affect them for years to come.

A lot of these young men already feel that they are being written-off, placed on the scrap heap, as I once did myself. What sort of a way is that to prevent crime? A lot of them come from appalling backgrounds and many of them have been the victims themselves of physical, sexual or emotional abuse. Their self-esteem is at rock bottom. Many of them have issues with drug dependency and a high proportion have somehow fallen through the education net. No wonder they commit crime. They have nothing more to lose, whilst in prison they do not have to think too hard unless they are challenged through well-conceived offending behaviour programmes.

My job is to try and change their outlook. The staff already make huge efforts to show them that they *can* turn their lives around and are encouraging them to use their time in custody in a constructive way. Many prisoners are undergoing vocational training aimed at increasing

---

[1] *The Ballad of Reading Gaol: The Story of a Most Famous Prison at the Time of Oscar Wilde, Before and After,* Anthony Stokes, Waterside Press (forthcoming).

their access to employment and there are various partnerships with local employers in an effort to further this. Others are obtaining educational qualifications. But one of the biggest hurdles they have to surmount when they get out is low self-esteem. Similarly there is their vulnerability to life on the street with all the temptations that this presents. A main focus of the staff is to try and get the inmates to believe in themselves and to resist the pressures that they will face to commit fresh offences on the outside after they are released. As it is many of them think that because they have criminal records it will be impossible to get a job or find someone with whom they can build a life. That is where I come in. I spend a morning telling these lads about my past life and what I am doing today.

Some of them say, 'It's alright for you, Bob, you're a one-off' and argue that they are different: forsaken, neglected and have already been dumped by society. I try to convince them otherwise. They are naturally sceptical about anyone who takes time out in their own spare time to come in and talk to them without being paid. They cannot quite understand it. I answer them by saying, 'It is true, I am very busy person and I do not like to waste my time on things that are not productive. That is the reason why I come to see you - as I know that there is a lot of potential in you guys'. I persist until it wears them down.

Sometimes the ice is broken if we talk - gradually perhaps with a touch of humour - about the raw deal we have all had from the entire system! Like the four Yorkshiremen in that memorable scene from one of the early Amnesty International concerts in the 'The Secret Policeman's

Ball' series, in which each in turn conjures up an ever more ghastly picture of his childhood to that described by the man speaking previously - in a never ending merry-go-round, a downward spiral of increasingly pitiful descriptions of how bad life has been. Then the young prisoners have to learn to stop feeling sorry for themselves. There are always some of them who feel that they *can* make a better life for themselves and who are willing to grasp the nettle. With the others you just have to work harder and harder still at it.

• • •

Every now and then I run into people from my former life. Habits die hard and some of them still treat me as the Bob that they once knew! I went to an old friend's sixtieth birthday party and there were lots of old acquaintances whom I had not seen for very many years. It was great to catch up on what they had been doing with their lives. Some were in long-term relationships with great kids and doing well in proper careers - and most had moved on in their lives. But I did notice that some of them kept harking back to the things we got up to all those years ago. They rarely talked about what they were doing *today* - as if they were caught in a time-warp. They would say things like, 'Hey, Bob, remember the time we were at the boxing club and we did a bit of this and a bit of that?' Some would refer to the 'skulduggery' they were involved in and there was the occasional nudge and wink: 'Come on, Bob, ... you're not really this upstanding guy we've heard about?'.

But I am. And to hear those people talk you would think that the time when they were up to no good was the best time of their lives. They had allowed themselves to become locked in the past. I would respond by saying, 'Yeah, they were good times'. But what I was really thinking was, 'No, I don't remember that as a positive experience' or 'I have done a thousand and one better things since then . . . My world is that of today and tomorrow - and my main focus is on how each day will be better than the one before'.

There was one guy who insisted that each time he saw me I was with a different girl. I tried to explain that I did have quite a few dates, but it never got off to a good start because each time I took a young lady out I would end up blind drunk and incapable of standing upright, never mind doing anything more! Invariably, my date would get a cab home on her own, leaving me comatose in some second-rate establishment. I am not sure that I want to reminisce about that any more than I suspect my old comrades are really proud of what they got up to.

I think the reason why some people want to fantasise about their past way of life is that they are not happy with their existing one. They are not fulfilled. There is a part of them, if the truth be known, that keeps telling them they have not reached their true potential. Do not get me wrong, there are things about the past that have been priceless - events and turnings that helped me to get where I am today. But I would not give tuppence to go through it all again. You have to move on in life.

I am not proud of some of the things I have done in the past and I will never forget them, or the victims that I created. I work every day in an effort to put some of that right. What *is* important is what I have learnt from it and how I can apply that to my life today and tomorrow. And how I can use that experience to benefit other people and the community I live in. It is a question of living in the here and now, not dwelling in, fantasising about or over-romanticising the past.

• • •

A good friend of mine happened to be Don Cockle, the boxer. In 1955 he fought for the World Heavyweight Title against the holder, the American, Rocky Marciano, in San Francisco. Don put up a brave fight, but was outclassed and knocked out in the ninth round. But you have to remember that Marciano had forty-nine fights in his career and did not lose a single one of them. He retired undefeated, a feat unequalled to this day at any weight. In my opinion, it made Don's achievement that much greater: staying nine rounds with Marciano.

Don himself had eighty professional fights, of which he won sixty-five, lost fourteen and drew one. He could have used that experience to help him live a marvellous life. He could have become a sports commentator or boxing writer. He had a wealth of knowledge. He would have made a first-rate after dinner speaker. There were any number of ways in which he could have succeeded after retiring from the ring. Even to get into the position to be a contender for the world title, you have to be unusually focused, ambitious and you need guts. But Don hung up his ambition along with his gloves. Instead of moving on to the next positive phase in his life, he began to go downhill. He ended up sitting on a barstool, telling stories of his glory days in return for the next pint. He became a fork-lift truck driver and drank himself to death at an early age.

What a contrast between Don and one of his contemporaries, Henry Cooper. Like Don, Henry was a contender for the world crown in 1966, at Highbury, the home of Arsenal Football Club in North London. He fought the young Cassius Clay (who later changed his name to

Mohammed Ali). The fight was stopped in the sixth round because Henry had a deep gash over his left eye, but only after he had twice put Ali on the canvas.

When Henry retired he become a TV commentator and later became 'Sir Henry'. 'There but for fortune', some people might say, but there was more to it than that. Unlike Don Cockle, Henry Cooper was able to reposition his thinking. He did not believe that his best times lay behind him. He could think 'outside the box' (or 'outside the ring', if you prefer). He reinvented himself and his popularity soared.

• • •

I was once in San Francisco giving a series of lectures and during one of my days off my hosts took me to the Redwood Forest. Some of the trees there are over a thousand years old and stand hundreds of feet tall. There is a story about some of the little green frogs that live there. One of the frogs is talking to his companions and tells them of his greatest ambition which is to climb the tallest tree. Many of the frogs start laughing at him and saying 'Come off it! You are a frog. No way can you ever climb one of those trees, you must be crazy even to think of it'.

Undeterred, the little frog manages to convince a few other frogs that they could climb the biggest tree and they agree a date when they will make the attempt. But news of the climb leaks out and on the day when the attempt is due onlookers gather at the foot of the chosen tree - even though many stay in bed convinced that the attempt is a waste of time and energy.

As the climb starts, the crowd begins to chant, 'Come down, come down: you are tiny little frogs and you cannot climb a great big tree'. One by one the climbing frogs begin to hear this discouragement and start to come down from the tree, until there is just the first little green frog left climbing. The crowd is still chanting, 'Come down, come down,' but he keeps going and before long he reaches the top - to the amazement of the throng below.

He then starts to make his way down and when he gets to the bottom the crowd is jubilant and cheer him home. 'How did you manage to do it, against all the odds?', he is asked.

'Pardon me,' he says, 'Can you speak more slowly . . . I'm stone deaf'! Having not heard the sceptics he had no idea of his limitations.

It was the same for me all those years ago once I had decided that life had to change. People might as well have shouted from the rooftops to tell me I was barmy, because I was deaf and did not hear them. I did not hear it when people said that a dunce could not complete a degree, that someone with dyslexia could not become an author, or that an ex-offender could not become a probation officer.

In the end, the most sceptical voices come from within ourselves: the voices of self-doubt and the 'mental tapes' that we replay in our heads. Now with Sue by my side and a host of friends, I hear even less than I did before when discouragement is in the air. What happens nowadays is that I concentrate on what I *have* achieved in carving out - from unpromising materials - a decent, honest and rewarding life. I will do everything to keep it that way and to that end Sue's belief in me and my faith in God are a constant source of support.

When I am visited by the ghosts of my past - mingling with the guests at a reception or during a visit to a school or prison - I just think how lucky I am that things have changed for the better - that I survived the wrong turnings and false values of my youth and am still here to tell the tale - and enjoy the simple things in life. Like taking Bizzo for a walk!

• • •

Like very many people nowadays, I spend a great deal of my time sitting in front of a computer. I use it to write pre-sentence reports for the courts on offenders, articles for the press and even this book. It helps someone who is dyslexic to have an automated spellcheck! Naturally, I receive all manner of communications from cyberspace, by which I mean, over the internet, including what are known as 'spam emails' which can clog up the system and contain viruses to gobble up all my hard work. But one of these got through without doing any damage - indeed quite the opposite. I do not know where it came from, or who the author was, but it encapsulates what I think I am trying to say about who and what you listen to and how you interpret the situations that you come up against in life. Turning things around may be hard work but it becomes second nature after a while!

> I am thankful for the teenager who is not doing dishes but watching TV, because that means he is at home and not on the streets.
>
> For the taxes that I pay, because it means that I am employed.
>
> For the mess to clear after a party because it means that I have been surrounded by friends.
>
> For the clothes that fit a little too snug, because it means I have enough to eat.
>
> For the shadow that watches me work, because it means I am out in the sunshine.
>
> For the lawn that needs mowing, windows that need cleaning, and gutters that need fixing, because it means I have a home.
>
> For all the complaining I hear about the Government, because it means I have freedom of speech.
>
> For the parking spot I find at the far end of the car park, because it means I am capable of walking and that I have been blessed with transport.
>
> For my huge heating bill, because it means I am warm.
>
> For the person behind me in church who sings off key, because it means that I can hear.
>
> For the pile of laundry and ironing, because it means I have clothes to wear.
>
> For the weariness and aching muscles at the end of the day, because it means I have been capable of working hard.
>
> For the alarm that goes off in the early morning hours, because it means that I am alive!